The Rewards of Fasting

Experiencing the Power and Affections of God

Mike Bickle
with Dana Candler

Forerunner Books
Kansas City, Missouri

FOreruNNer BOOHS Ⓕ

The Rewards of Fasting: Experiencing the Power and Affections of God
By Mike Bickle with Dana Candler

Published by Forerunner Books
International House of Prayer–Kansas City
3535 East Red Bridge Road
Kansas City, Missouri 64137
(816) 763-0200 Ext. 675
www.IHOP.org

ISBN: 0-9776738-1-2

Unless otherwise noted, all Scripture quotations are from the New King James Version of the Bible. Copyright © 1979, 1980, 1982 by Thomas Nelson, Inc., publishers. Used by permission.

Scripture quotations marked KJV are from the King James Version of the Bible.

Scripture quotations marked NAS are from the New American Standard Bible. Copyright © 1960, 1962, 1963, 1968, 1971, 1972, 1973, 1975, 1977 by the Lockman Foundation. Used by permission.

Scripture quotations marked NIV are from the Holy Bible, New International Version. Copyright © 1973, 1978, 1984, International Bible Society. Used by permission.

Cover design by Steve Willis, Underpin Design
Interior design by Dale Jimmo

Printed in the United States of America

TABLE OF CONTENTS

TABLE OF CONTENTS

FOREWORD

"Fasting." The word alone can seem a bit overwhelming and the act completely unapproachable. However, as that slight shiver at the thought of fasting runs down your spine, I encourage you all the more to dive into the realities found within this book. There is truth to be had, and mysteries to be found within these pages. "The Rewards of Fasting" is a practical introduction to the glory found in something that has been lost in our time.

The idea of voluntary sacrifice is rare and has been lost in our culture of entertainment, gratification and pleasure. Especially in the lifestyle of the average young adult, there is a constant search for pleasure. We have everything and anything at our fingertips, and the whirlwind of possibilities only leaves us disillusioned and unsatisfied. In our dissatisfaction, we run to another "best" thing, only to come out more dissatisfied and searching all the harder. We have submerged ourselves in an age of ease and comfort, and have lost several foundational principles of the Christian life. I believe fasting is one of these principles.

While living a lifestyle of fasting, or even doing a one-time run of fasting, is often regarded as "radical," I believe the opposite is true. Fasting is Christianity 101. Fasting is not only for the radical.

It is not only for the extremist. It is not only for the religious saint. In fact, the results of fasting expose weakness and humility. Denying our desires and basic needs causes us to be more aware of our humanity and frailty. We realize how futile we are, but how great God is. In times of fasting, we come to grips with our true nature and remember once again how infinite our Source is.

So, no ... fasting is not for the strong. It is not for the solid. It is not for the perfect. Fasting is for the common, weak, frail, ordinary individual who realizes his or her lack and has a desperate need for more of God. The realities of fasting truly are a bit bizarre. It doesn't make sense to our natural minds how sacrificing food and pleasures unlocks our hearts and minds to receive more of God Himself, but the set-up of His kingdom is perfect. Why did God set it up this way? His nature and character are to be found in asking such questions, and I encourage you to ask them as you read this book. Ask questions as you dive into the knowledge of fasting and He will reveal bits of the mystery and lead you further into cultivating a lifestyle where it is consistently walked out.

You guys, this is our glory! It is our glory to say "no" to the fleeting earthly pleasures that surround us in the here and now. God has given us an opportunity to choose Him on this side of eternity, above all lesser things. Fasting is more than denying ourselves food. It isn't really about being hungry. While we do get hungry when we fast, fasting is really about experiencing more of God. When we are physically weak from not eating, we become more sensitive to God and the things of God. We experience Jesus on a deeper level. It is about choosing voluntary weakness so that Christ may abound even more within us. Fasting is the road to revelation and encounter that we cannot receive any other way.

I want to encourage you as you begin this journey. Maybe you've had fasting as a part of your life for a long time. Maybe you've fasted a few times and want to know more. Maybe you've tried once or twice and felt you failed. Maybe you've never even heard of fasting. Wherever you are, I commend you for getting this far. The mere fact that you have an interest in fasting shows your hunger for God. I am excited for where He will take you and what will be unlocked as you walk into the fullness of what He has for you.

We are all on the same playing field. We are all broken. We are all weak. We are all desperate for more of God. Talk to Him; ask Him what and how you are to fast; and then pray for His grace, knowing that He loves that you are simply after more of Him. Fasting is not scary ... it is the Christian lifestyle. This should be a practical life discipline of every believer. It is not as hard as we think it is. It is attainable for the ordinary, average, weak, pizza-loving 20-something person. We can all enter into the fasted lifestyle ... and I'm sure you will see it make a huge difference in your life.

This book is part of a series of "Onething Reality" books. The goal of the "Onething Reality" book series is to provide foundational biblical teaching on topics that are essential to every Christian's life in God and that are core realities of Onething Ministries. As a ministry of the International House of Prayer Missions Base, Onething Ministries shares the same core values and realities of IHOP-KC and publishes "Onething Reality" books as a means of sharing those core values with the Body of Christ.

I pray that as you read this book you will be moved and encouraged to embrace the "Fasted Lifestyle." I pray you will take to heart the message that fasting is a God-given gift, intended by God to bring us into a deeper revelation and experience of His power, love, affections and emotions.

Dwayne Roberts
Director of Onething Ministries
International House of Prayer Missions Base
Kansas City, Missouri

INTRODUCTION

I believe there are people alive on Earth right now who will witness the Second Coming of Jesus. While no one knows the day or the hour of His coming, the Bible says that we are to know the season of His coming (1 Thess. 5:1-6). Jesus may return in 10 years or it may be 50. I assume it is closer to 50 than 10, but regardless of the actual number of years, I believe we are at the beginning of the final generation. The Bible reveals a significant amount of prophetic information about the generation that will see His return. God will pour out His glory and release His judgments in an unprecedented way in that time. Jesus is zealous for His Church and will lead her to victory, even in the midst of a world torn apart by the rage of Satan, the escalating sin of men and women, and the judgments of God.

The Holy Spirit is readying the Bride of Christ—the Body of Christ—at this time for the coming days of glory and opposition. How radically the Lord must change the Church to prepare her for His return! What the Western Church today accepts as normal values and practices will be dramatically altered as our minds are renewed and we are transformed into the people God originally designed us to be.

How do we prepare to experience the fullness of what God is about to release? How do we cooperate with the Holy Spirit as

He leads us into the same intimacy and power seen in the New Testament Church? Just as it was for the first-century saints and for the Church throughout the ages, living what we at the International House of Prayer call "the fasted lifestyle" will be integral to this process.

By definition, fasting is abstaining from food. The fast that we are after, however, goes far beyond just denying ourselves physical nourishment. Our desire is to position our hearts to encounter Jesus as the Bridegroom God. Throughout history people have often fasted with a wrong focus, seeking to earn God's favor and attention. But we can never manipulate God. We can embrace extreme self-debasements in our desire to prove our dedication to Him, but this is not what God is after. What He delights in is our obedience and our pursuit of intimacy with Him. More important to Him than fasting is that we do His will. The Lord spoke through Samuel the prophet, saying that it is better to obey God than to offer Him a special sacrifice (1 Sam. 15:22-23).

How, then, should we approach fasting during this urgent time? When we fast it must be as a means to an end rather than as an end in itself. We do not fast to prove anything to God or to earn His favor. The eastern religions practice fasting that is preoccupied with self, as their followers seek to earn God's blessing, but the Scripture teaches us to fast to strengthen us in our quest to be preoccupied with God and His will.

Regular fasting is part of the normal Christian life. It is Christianity 101. In Matthew 6:16, Jesus used the phrase, "*When* you fast" (not *if* you fast), implying that fasting was meant to occur in the normal course of any disciple's life. Jesus promised that God would openly reward those who approach fasting with the right spirit (Matt. 6:18). Fasting is a grace that significantly increases our receptivity to the Lord's voice and His Word. It allows us to enter into depths in our relationships with God that are beyond what we normally experience. We fast in order to encounter God more intimately and more profoundly and to change the world.

In Isaiah 58, God ordained fasting to (1) loosen the bonds of wickedness in our lives; (2) undo heavy burdens in the lives of others; (3) help the oppressed be set free as we minister to them by the anointing of the Spirit; (4) break every yoke of the religious spirit; (5) give bread to the hungry and provide the poor with housing; (6) allow the light of revelation in God's Word to break forth in us like the morning; (7) allow our emotional and physical health to speedily spring forth; (8) cause righteousness to break forth in the places where we struggle; and (9) cause the glory and power of the Lord to operate in our ministries.

I call believers to fast at least one day a week. It is better to fast two days a week. This is well within the reach of most people. We desperately need more revelation of Jesus as our Bridegroom who has burning desire for us and fiery affections toward us. As we live in the truth of the bridal paradigm, we fast because we long for Jesus. Jesus told the Pharisees the day would come when the Bridegroom would be taken away from the disciples, and then they would fast out of longing for Him (Matt. 9:15). When Jesus ascended to Heaven after His death and resurrection, He was taken away in the sense indicated in this Scripture. The Bride of Christ is meant to long for His return, His Second Coming, and fasting is one way we express this longing.

My hope is that this book will help equip you to embrace the discipline, grace and joy of fasting, so that you might encounter the fullness of all God, as your heavenly Bridegroom, has for you.

Mike Bickle
Director, International House of Prayer Missions Base
Kansas City, Missouri

CHAPTER ONE

The Bridegroom God

Several years ago, if you had spoken about fasting to a gathering of believers, you would more than likely have found the response to be mostly one of disconnect and general disinterest. They would have considered fasting to be a secondary subject, an optional Christian discipline, one exercise among a host of others. Today, however, I see this collective response declining among Christians. There is a growing hunger and desperation that flows from the Body of Christ's recognition that we are spiritually barren. We understand that we are in great need of the in-breaking of God's love and power. As a result, there is clearly a growing enthusiasm for fasting, even fasting as a lifestyle.

This new interest in fasting is God's gift to the Body of Christ. It is part of God's commitment to prepare the Church for the soon coming time of glory and crisis in the End Times. This ready response is surely the work of God in our midst. And it is unmistakably in line with the Word of God. With boldness Jesus emphasized that the Father rewards fasting (Matt. 6:17, 18). This proclamation alone makes fasting of great importance to the true followers of Jesus. It is not secondary. The grace of fasting must not be neglected.

There is a tension in fasting and living the fasted lifestyle. While God does reward fasting, the rewards He gives are not earned or deserved by us because of our fasting. We are weak people who can never earn God's favor or rewards, but can only receive them. We give ourselves to the grace of fasting by positioning ourselves before His infinite goodness. He wants to flood our lives with many rewards—rewards that are internal as our hearts encounter Him, external as our circumstances are touched by His power, and eternal as fasting impacts even our eternal rewards.

Truly the rewards that the Father gives to those who fast regularly are vast. And that is why, even now, He is preparing the hearts of believers worldwide to say "yes" to the New Testament lifestyle of prayer and fasting. He will prepare us as we experience Jesus' affection as our Bridegroom God. Our ability to experience more of our glorious God is deeply connected to our embracing the grace of fasting.

Our Dilemma: We Need To Experience God's Love

Deep within the human heart is the desire to know that we are loved and valued. We feel the pain of loneliness and rejection so profoundly because God designed our spirits for the exhilaration of being loved and loving in return. The longing for acceptance, the ache for love, is one of the primary driving forces in our lives. Yet we have a strong dilemma. The dilemma is that though our desire for love is real, and though we are innately designed by God to be exhilarated by His love and acceptance of us, there remains a distance between the knowledge of this love and our actual experience of it. Believe it or not, fasting is one of the most practical ways to posture our hearts to experience more of God's affection and love. Traditionally, many people have thought of fasting as a spiritual discipline practiced to avert a crisis, or as a posture of repentance before God. One of the main reasons God gave us this grace has to do with love and our ability to experience the rewards of that love.

The gap between knowing that God loves us and actually experiencing that love is rooted in living from a false identity based on the way people receive us, rather than on how God receives us. How we think and feel about ourselves is greatly impacted by those whose opinions we value most. From the time we are born, our sense of personal identity and value is shaped by what our parents, friends and acquaintances think of us. However, our Creator is the only One who fully knows who we were designed to be. He tells us who we really are by revealing how much He loves us. Our belief in His affection for us determines how we feel about ourselves, how we approach life, how we interact with others, and how we deal with setbacks and difficulties. God wants our identity and sense of value to be rooted and grounded in the knowledge of His affections for us (Eph. 3:17-18). This is where our hearts come alive!

How is it that Jesus feels so much for us? In His final public message before going to the cross (Matt. 22:1-14), Jesus revealed what was burning in His heart. He described the Kingdom of God as a wedding, and the Father as the One arranging a glorious marriage for His Son (Matt. 22:2). This is the highest revelation of the Kingdom of God. It is the revelation of Jesus as our Bridegroom God and of us as His cherished Bride. It is through receiving and taking to heart this revelation that the gap is closed and the dilemma is solved in our experience of God's love. Therefore, we must encounter Jesus as our Bridegroom God by positioning our hearts and lives in such a way that this revelation really takes root in us.

The Church's Bridal Identity

The apostle John prophesied of the time at the end of the age when the Spirit and the Bride would cry out, "Come, Lord Jesus" (Rev. 22:17). It is one of the most important prophecies describing the activities and experiences of the end-time Church. The Holy Spirit will trumpet the message of Jesus as a passionate Bridegroom and the identity of the Church as His cherished Bride. The Holy Spirit's final emphasis before Jesus' Second Coming will be on the intimate relationship between Him and His Bride. John described the Church as being in deep unity with the Holy Spirit at that time, saying and doing what the Spirit is saying and doing. The Holy Spirit will have revealed the Church's core identity. Instead of being called the "Church," she will have completely assumed her identity as the "Bride" and will be fully participating in the bridal longing for the Bridegroom to "come," to return.

This final prophecy reveals not only what the Holy Spirit's primary activities will be in the coming days, but also three key things that will happen in and through the Church. First, the Church will be anointed with the Spirit. The Spirit will rest on the Church in great power and revelation. Second, the Church will be deeply engaged in intercession, crying out "Come, Lord Jesus." Third, the Church will be established in her bridal identity. Yes, we are and always will be His army, His family, His body, His Kingdom, His sons and daughters, and much more. However, we are approaching the first time in history when the Holy Spirit will emphasize the Church's spiritual identity as Jesus' Bride. When we speak of these truths, we sometimes refer to them as the "bridal paradigm" of the Kingdom of God.

The Bridal Paradigm of the Kingdom of God

The word "paradigm" means perspective or view. The bridal paradigm views the Kingdom through the eyes of a Bride whose love is loyal, wholehearted and devoted. It is the "bridal perspective" of the Kingdom of God.

Being the Bride of Christ is not about being male or female, but about all believers being given a position of indescribable privilege far beyond even what angels enjoy. It is an invitation to experience God's affection and desire for us. As sons of God, heirs of His power, we are given a position that allows us to experience God's throne (Rev. 3:21; Rom. 8:17). As His Bride, we are in a position to experience God's heart—His emotions, affections, and desire—for us.

As women are the sons of God, so men are the Bride of Christ. Both describe a position of privilege before God that transcends gender. Most Christian women do not struggle with the idea of being sons of God because they do not see it as a call to be less feminine. However, men often struggle with being the Bride of Christ because they wrongly conclude it is a call to be less masculine. They cannot relate to being Jesus' Bride, thinking that they should picture themselves wearing a wedding dress. We must understand that being His Bride points to a position of privileged nearness that enables us to encounter His heart.

Some of the greatest men of God functioned in the foundational reality of the bridal identity, which is intimacy with God. King David was Israel's greatest warrior, yet he was a lovesick worshipper, ravished by God's desire for him and fascinated by God's beauty (Ps. 27:4). Being a "man after God's own heart" implies that David was a student of the emotions of God's heart.

Jesus called John the apostle a "Son of Thunder" because of his fiery personality (Mark 3:17). He was the one who wanted to call fire down on a Samaritan city (Luke 9:54). John was a rough and rugged guy, yet the Bible Indicates how he saw himself. Five times he described himself as the disciple whom Jesus loved (John 13:23; 19:26; 20:2; 21:7; 21:20). It's easy to see that what was most important to John was that he was the one who laid his head on the Lord's breast (John 21:20).

John the Baptist ate locusts, wore camel skin, and called the Pharisees outrageous names like "brood of vipers." Jesus said he was the "greatest man born of a woman" (Matt. 11:11). What empowered this powerful prophet was the revelation he had of Jesus as the Bridegroom God. John spoke of hearing the voice of the Bridegroom (John 3:29) as that which caused his heart to be overwhelmed with joy.

King David, the Apostle John and John the Baptist all walked in deep intimacy with God. In this way they experienced the core reality of what it means to be the Bride of Christ. Their intimacy with God did not undermine their masculinity, but rather strengthened and established it. The way we view ourselves is greatly impacted when we understand Jesus as a passionate Bridegroom. We begin to see ourselves as ones who have immense value to Him, just as a cherished bride does to her husband. These truths result in our hearts being enraptured and overcome by His love. We become lovesick. The Bride in Song of Solomon twice spoke of being lovesick for God (Song 2:5; 5:8).

The Bridegroom Message

The Bridegroom message is a call to active intimacy with God. Paul taught that the Spirit searches the deep things of God, so that He might reveal them to us (1 Cor. 2:10-12). God has invited each of us to experience the deep things of His heart. He has opened Himself up for us to understand and feel His emotions, desires and affections. This is foundational to what Paul prayed for the Church when he asked that we would be able to comprehend the depth of God's love (Eph. 3:18-19). It is as we discover the depths of God's affection, little by little, combined with the grace of fasting, that we begin to touch the internal rewards promised to us by Jesus (Matt. 6:17, 18). We become exhilarated on the inside in the wake of this reality.

What is the depth of His love? What are Jesus' emotions? First, let's consider that He is filled with tender mercy. In other words, He is gentle with us in our weakness. He is tender with us in our spiritual immaturity. Some people confuse immaturity with rebellion. In their immaturity, they imagine God is angry with them as if they were rebellious. It is true that God is angry at rebellion, but he has a heart of tenderness toward sincere believers who, though immature and weak, seek to obey Him. He enjoys us even in our weakness. This is the profound truth that we must grasp. During the time of his youth, David said that God delivered him because He delighted in him (Ps. 18:19). David was not a spiritually mature man when he wrote Psalm 18. In the same Psalm, he proclaimed that God's gentleness made him great (Ps. 18:35). David did not fear that God would treat him harshly because of his weaknesses. God actually enjoys us in our weakness; He feels pleasure over us while we are growing, not just after we've matured.

Second, Jesus' heart is filled with gladness. He has a happy heart, a heart happier than any man in history. God anointed Jesus with the oil of gladness more than any of His companions or His fellow human beings (Heb. 1:9). Traditionally, many people have viewed God as being mostly mad or mostly sad when He relates to them. The truth confounds us—Jesus is mostly glad when He interacts with sincere believers. Even in our weakness we can approach Him and be confident that He is glad to relate to us.

Third, Jesus' emotions are filled with fiery affections for us. Jesus feels about us the same way the Father feels about Him (John 15:9). This is stunning! The second Person of the Trinity feels about broken human beings the same way that the first Person of the Trinity feels about Him. The depth of the Father's love for Jesus is unfathomable, and we share in the very same love. It seems unthinkable, but the Bible tells us it is true.

Fourth, Jesus the Bridegroom is zealous. Love is not passive and the God of affection is an all-consuming fire (Deut. 4:24). His jealousy for us is as demanding as the grave, a most powerful flame, the very flame of God (Song. 8:6, 7). With fierce zeal He consumes all that hinders love in us, everything that gets in the way. He will not have only a portion of our hearts. He wants the entirety of our hearts and He will continue to jealously pursue every aspect of our lives until we are fully His. Out of His zeal come His judgments, which destroy all that opposes love and all that injures His Church (Prov. 6:34; Ezek. 38:18-19; Zech. 1:14, 8:2; Rev. 19:2). The Lord is zealous for His people with great zeal and with great fervor (Zech. 8:1-2).

Our Lovesick God

At the core of the Bridegroom message are Jesus' emotions for us and His commitments to us as a lovesick God. The God who created Heaven and Earth is a Bridegroom whose heart burns in holy love for His Bride. The God who possesses all power desires intimacy with human beings. God's bridegroom nature is a dramatic and significant reality. I do not know of anything that brings a person's life and identity into greater clarity than the realization that Jesus has fiery affections for him or her. This paradigm of the Kingdom has a profound impact on us, utterly transforming us from within. Only when we understand Jesus' great desire for us can we understand who we really are. We are His eternal companions. He shares with us that which the Father has given Him. He shares with us His heart.

The King of kings is a God of indescribable passion. That this passion burns hot with love for you and me is a powerful truth that is intended to define our lives. Our human emotions are radically transformed when we see Jesus as a passionate Bridegroom God and ourselves as His beloved Bride. If we do not feel loved and in love, we are spiritually bored and are thus more vulnerable to compromise, lacking in courage and strength. On the other hand, when we come face to face with the extravagant affections of God, the very core of our being is impacted. This internal impact is what we are after. It is what changes our lives.

Living according to the reality of Jesus being our heavenly Bridegroom and viewing ourselves as His cherished Bride is the only way we can prepare for the Lord's return. It is our only hope of filling the void of our loneliness and rejection. Yet we are not naturally aware of these truths. We do not naturally live in this identity, though it is the highest revelation of who we are before Him. Currently, the revelation of Jesus as the Bridegroom is not commonly understood by the Church. However, the Lord has a plan to awaken the people of God. He will unveil Himself to them as a Bridegroom and He will do it through prayer and fasting. Jesus invites us to know Him as our Bridegroom and to experience the rewards of prayer and fasting. God beckons us to come near Him. Oh, that we would respond to this invitation wholeheartedly.

Responding to the Bridegroom

By knowing Jesus as our Bridegroom and seeing ourselves as His Bride, we will become energized with a spirit of prayer and filled with courage to live lives abandoned to God in holiness. Only then will fasting seem appropriate, reasonable or even wise. The only logical response to God's extravagant love for us is one of wholehearted love, characterized by denying ourselves. As we do, we will lay hold of the highest things God has for us. This present age is but a brief window in eternity. In light of eternity, this life is but one small "moment" we have to respond in full obedience and love to Jesus. In loving Him, we seek to obey Him at any cost. In responding to His love, we receive all that He longs to pour into our lives. Jesus said that if we love Him we will keep His commandments, but if we do not keep them, our love is not genuine (John 14:15, 23-24).

His first command is to love God with all our heart (Matt. 22:37). The western Church does not presently put this commandment in its rightful place, but the Holy Spirit will use the revelation of Jesus as the Bridegroom God to restore it to the first place in our lives. Before the Lord returns, the Church worldwide will be passionately in love with God and living abandoned lifestyles of happy holiness. The lovesick God will be worshiped by a Bride who is also lovesick.

How do we grow from immature love to blazing, abandoned love for God? We dive headlong into the revelation of His desire for us. It is that simple. It is so simple, in fact, that it seems almost too good to believe. In faith, we must receive the testimony of His unyielding affection for us, even in our weakness, and this will empower us to run toward God when we fail, instead of running away from Him. In the midst of our failure, we must remember that our God is a God of gladness who loves us *and likes us,* not a God who is quick to anger and who is continually disappointed with us. Our love for Him will grow as we take to heart this foundational principle regarding His feelings for us.

It is the indescribable beauty of Jesus, the Bridegroom God, that fascinates our hearts just as it did David's. David desired one thing above all: to behold God's beauty (Ps. 27:4). As we enter more deeply into the understanding of God's love for us, our desire to live "lives of one thing," governed by the first commandment, will grow and expand. Inevitably, we will begin to eagerly hope for continuing revelation of His heart, for deeper understanding of our bridal identity, and for greater experience of His unchangeable love. We will hunger for more of Him.

The grace of fasting is God's answer to our cry for "more." Fasting enlarges our capacity to receive truth, and accelerates the process of God's truths taking root in our own hearts. It is a God-given way to make room for more of God and therefore is an essential component to the age-old question of "How do I grow in love for God?" In order to grow in love, our capacity for God must increase, and in order for our capacity to increase, we need to incorporate the practice of fasting into our lives. Fasting fuels our experience of God's love. This profound truth is the heart of this book. We must understand the scriptural foundations of what we call the "Bridegroom fast," which is energized by the Body of Christ's encounter with Jesus as the Bridegroom God. In the next chapter, we will look at the different types of fasts the Bible sets forth, including the Bridegroom fast.

CHAPTER TWO

Seven Types of Biblical Fasting

When I first came to know the Lord as a young man, I did not like fasting at all. I loved worship and teaching gatherings, but I hated prayer and fasting. As I read books on these subjects, however, I began to see that God has set up His Kingdom to work best when His people pray and fast. I did not like that idea. You could not have convinced me that one day I would be preaching and writing books on these subjects—they were my least favorite things to do.

Many times I set my heart to spend the day in fasting and prayer, but within a few short hours I was ready to quit, complaining to God, "Why? Why did You set up Your Kingdom this way? I don't understand! Why do You want me to sit here doing nothing except telling You what You already know and not eating? What is the point of this? What is the wisdom of this? God, I could be doing so much for You! I could be impacting many people if You would just let me *do* something instead of wasting my life away in prayer and fasting." Nothing seemed more foolish or more wasteful to me, but God wanted me to understand that this truly was the way of wisdom and the way that His power would most effectively be released in my heart and ministry.

The Power of Prayer and Fasting

God has set up His Kingdom in such a way that some things that seem the weakest to people are actually the most powerful before God. The natural mind argues, why prayer and fasting? After all, it is telling God what He already knows, while not eating food. Without the mindset of Christ, it is difficult to understand the wisdom of a lifestyle of prayer and fasting. Yet there is truly nothing more powerful to which we could give our lives. God's Kingdom is governed by prayer. When we give ourselves to prayer and fasting, it affects the spiritual realm, even the activity of angels and demons.

Prayer transcends time and distance. The apostle Paul could impact and bring change to the Church in Ephesus by praying while he was far away in a prison in Rome. In fact, the place of prayer is the governmental center of the universe, but the reality is that the spirit of prayer is foreign to the human spirit unless we are experiencing God's grace (Zech. 12:10). The Christian life requires cooperation with God in His grace.

God will not do our part and we cannot do His part. If we do not do our part, some of the help and blessing that God would have given us are withheld. Our part includes making quality decisions to deny ourselves (say no to sin and pride); to feed our spirit on the Word; to ask for Divine help and intervention through prayer with fasting; and to embrace godly activities (ministry, service) and relationships. God's part includes releasing supernatural influences on our hearts (power, wisdom, desires); on our bodies (healing); on our circumstances (provision, protection, direction); and on our relationships (favor).

God governs the universe in intimate partnership with His people through intercession. He has chosen to give His people a dynamic role in determining some of our quality of life, based on our response to the grace of God, particularly in prayer, fasting, obedience and meekness. God opens doors of blessing and closes doors of oppression in response to prayer. There are blessings that He has chosen to give, but only if His people rise up in the partnership of prayer to ask for them. James said that we do not have because we do not ask in prayer (James 4:2). And Jesus spoke of demons that would not stop tormenting people until driven out by prayer and fasting (Matt. 17:21).

There are three steps in our partnership with God. First, *God initiates* what He wants by declaring it in His Word and stirring our hearts to believe for it. Second, *we respond* in obedience with prayer and fasting. Third, *God answers* our response by releasing that for which we have cried out. Our prayers matter greatly, even when we do not feel their power. Some people "trust" the sovereignty of God in a non-biblical way by "trusting" God to do the role He has assigned to us. This is not trust; it is presumption. It is true that His big plan for the broad strokes of history will not be thwarted, but there are many things that God will not give us individually until we pursue them in faith and obedience.

The foundation of intercession, which is a form of prayer, is to say back to God what He first says to us, either from Scripture or from personal prophetic information given to us by the Holy Spirit (1 Tim. 1:18). Prayer causes us to internalize God's Word as we speak His ideas back to Him. Each time we say back to God what He has declared to us, it marks our spirit, illuminates our mind and tenderizes our heart. Our character is transformed. All this happens as we engage in intercession, because God's words are spirit and life (John 6:63). God's requirement that we pray reflects His desire for intimate partnership and connection with us.

Prayer and fasting are spiritual weapons we use to actively resist Satan. Our war is both physical and spiritual. Paul said we do not wrestle against flesh and blood, but against principalities and against spiritual hosts (armies) of wickedness. Therefore, we should take up the whole armor of God so that we may be able to quench all the flaming missiles of the wicked one by praying always (Eph. 6:12-18). The weapons of our warfare are not fleshly but spiritual (2 Cor. 10:3-5). We must actively resist the supernatural, fiery missiles Satan directs against us (James 4:6-7; 1 Pet. 5:8-9). In our war against sin and darkness, it is not enough to only do the physical outward activities of resisting sin or ministering to others. We must also engage in the spiritual part of this war by actively resisting Satan through prayer with fasting.

The Foundational Principles of Biblical Fasting

To understand the power that God releases through prayer and fasting, we must consider some foundational principles. First, *fasting is an invitation*. God invites us to fast because He wants us to want more of Him. The nature of true desire to be with someone requires that we not be forced to desire them. It must be voluntary. God *invites us* so that the voluntary aspect is preserved. We can still be saved and go to Heaven without ever fasting or knowing God more intimately; however, if we say "yes" to Him in fasting, God uses this response as a doorway to bring us into greater measures of encountering His heart. There are blessings that will only be released when our spiritual hunger reaches the point that we want to fast in order to receive more of God. He rewards hunger and imparts more grace to those who are hungry for more of Him.

自相矛盾 The second principle is that *fasting is a paradox.* When we fast, the props we use to stimulate ourselves are removed; the things that give us the illusion of strength are temporarily gone. Sometimes when fasting, we feel raw before God as we become even more aware of our sinful motives and passions. The paradox is that as we experience the pain of this rawness, our spirit is tenderized. Our bodies are weak and hungry, but our spirit-man is more sensitive to the Holy Spirit. In all this, our resolve is strengthened to live wholly for God. The paradox of fasting is that as we experience weakness in our flesh, we are strengthened in our spirit.

Third, *fasting is a grace*. We will sustain a life of fasting only by God's grace, not by our own strength. Fasting is more than gritting our teeth as we endure it. Instead, we ask God for grace to enter into the mystery of connecting with Him in fasting. As we embrace the voluntary weakness of fasting, we receive more spiritual strength in our walk with God. His grace multiplies to those who pursue it (2 Pet. 1:2; 3:18).

God truly does give grace to fast—even to people in our day who live in the modern Western culture. I want to expose the lie that 21st century believers cannot fast like the believers in the days of old. This is a lie that breeds passivity toward this powerful gift. We dull our consciences with the lie that since our "pace of life" is so rapid, regular fasting is not practical. Beloved, there has never been a society less physically challenged on a day-to-day basis than this one. Modern conveniences assure us a sedentary existence, compared with previous generations, and most of us have to invent ways to exert ourselves. We tell ourselves that fasting is too hard, and that we will be too tired and uncomfortable, when in actuality the *fear of fasting* is far worse than the fasting itself.

被動

God designed our bodies to operate at their best with regular fasting. Our bodies are actually cleansed and strengthened in the process of fasting. I recommend an approach to the fasted lifestyle that includes setting aside regular fast days each week, rather than occasional short or long fasts. As we fast on a regular basis, a change in our mindset and the rhythm of our bodies begins to set in. This is one expression of the grace of fasting. It is similar to working out. When we don't exercise regularly, it is difficult to get started. It takes time and consistent exercise before we begin to adjust. It is the same with fasting on a regular basis.

There is no easier time than right now to say "yes" to this grace and to partner with God in it, to develop a history in prayer and fasting. Certainly, as the pressure at the end of the age increases, a greater percentage of Christians will enter into the grace of fasting than ever before.

The fourth principle of fasting is that *fasting is humbling.* Scripture describes fasting as "humbling" to or "afflicting" one's soul (Is. 58:3, 5). David spoke of fasting as one way he humbled himself before God (Ps. 35:13; 69:10). Our bodies are tired, our minds are spacey, we are not operating at full capacity, and weakness seems

spaced-out
迷迷糊糊的

to pervade everything to which we put our hands. Suddenly we find ourselves unable to do even the most normal tasks well—things we have always taken for granted. Beloved, there is no question: it humbles us to fast. This is how God planned it.

The fifth principle is that *fasting is worship.* Only weak people fast and pray; only those who recognize their need for more of God fast. Fasting unto the Lord is a declaration of our great need of Him. We fast out of desire to be better equipped to pour out our lives fully to Him. This is precious to the Lord. When God's people humble

lk in greater purity, God

ys, "I urge you ... to offer

pleasing to God—this is

The Seven Types of Biblical Fasting

There are seven categories of fasting found in the Bible. Fasting could be categorized in many different ways; this is just one of many ways. These seven different forms of fasting are responses to different circumstances and unique motivations. Note that these categories will often overlap with each other. Some of these are rooted in the Old Testament but continue to be necessary in the New Testament Church.

1. Fasting to experience the power of God *in personal ministry*

We can fast for a greater release of God's power in our ministry. There are many biblical examples of this type of fast. When the disciples could not set a demonized boy free, Jesus told them that the demon involved was the kind that would not go out except by prayer and fasting (Matt. 17:21). The great power with which John the Baptist preached was undoubtedly connected to his fasted lifestyle (Matt. 11:18). The same can be said of the power that was seen in the apostle Paul's ministry. Fasting was a regular part of his life (Acts 9:9; 2 Cor. 6:5, 11:27).

The early Church fasted twice a week, on Wednesdays and Fridays, to experience more power with God. Throughout Church history, many anointed men and women have practiced regular fasting as they led great revivals. Commenting on the leaders of revival in history, Andrew Murray, the famous South African Church leader, said that we could learn much from these anointed leaders, who dedicated themselves to God by separating themselves from the spirit and pleasures of the world, through regular fasting with prayer.

Charles Finney was one of the most powerful preachers in America's history. A tremendous anointing of conviction rested on his preaching. He reported leading more than 500,000 people to the Lord in an eight-week period during the great New York revival of 1857. Finney wrote that when the grace of prayer left him, his preaching became as weak as other men. When this happened, he would spend several days in prayer and fasting, until the spirit of prayer returned, along with power on his preaching. He proclaimed that the power on his preaching was connected to regular times of prayer with fasting. Finney wrote, "I was led into a state of great dissatisfaction with my own lack of faith and love. I felt myself weak in temptation and needed frequently to hold days of fasting and prayer in order to retain communion with God that would enable me to work in revival with power."

Many well-known preachers of the past exemplified this same principle. They were blessed with an unusual anointing of the Spirit that always included special power on their preaching for soul winning. In some cases, they were anointed with signs and wonders. Examples include George Whitfield, Jonathan Edwards, David Brainerd, Charles Wesley, Marie Woodworth-Etter, and Aimee Simple McPherson.

One of the most outstanding examples of a person whose life illustrates the connection between much fasting and prayer and the release of signs and wonders is John G. Lake, who ministered in the early 1900's. The Lord stirred this insurance man from Chicago to pray and fast until he experienced several major breakthroughs of power in his preaching and in signs and wonders. God released unusually powerful miracles through him for many years. He went to South Africa for five years and birthed hundreds of churches, seeing an estimated 500,000 healings, which included people being raised from the dead. He led untold thousands of people to Christ in those days.

Mahesh Chavda, a contemporary example, went on two 40-day water fasts a year for ten years. The Lord has released unusual miracles in his ministry, using him several times to raise the dead and to open blind eyes. He is particularly known for being anointed with authority over demons.

The Lord is looking for people today who will seek Him with all of their hearts. He can entrust such people with His power. He spoke prophetically to one man in our midst, saying that to a people without mixture, He would give the Spirit without measure. The fasted lifestyle is an important part of our pursuit to be such a people in this hour.

2. Fasting for prophetic revelation of the End Times

We are living in the generation in which God will raise up men and women of unusual prophetic insight. There will be an unprecedented release of prophetic revelation in the Church before Jesus returns (Acts 2:17-21). Daniel prophesied that in the End Times God would raise up "people with prophetic understanding" who would teach multitudes (Dan. 11:33-35; 12:4, 10). These prophetic people will stand in the very counsel of the Lord with mature understanding of what He is doing in the time of judgment. "For who has stood in the counsel of the Lord, and has perceived and heard His word? ... The anger of the Lord will not turn back until He has executed and performed the thoughts of His heart. In the latter days you will understand it perfectly" (Jer. 23:18-20).

And those of the people who understand shall instruct many ... And some of those of understanding shall fall (martyrdom), to refine them, purify them, and make them white, until the time of the end; because it is still for the appointed time (Dan. 11:33-35).

God answered Daniel's fierce determination to be a man of prophetic understanding. When the prophet set his face toward God with fasting and prayer, he was given revelation of Israel's destiny at the end of the age (Dan. 9:1-3, 20-23; 10:1-3, 12-14). After he had prayed and fasted for twenty-one days, he was visited by an angel who told him that his prayers had been heard from the first day that he had set his heart to understand and to humble himself before God (Dan. 10:10-12). While Daniel was in prayer, the angel Gabriel came to give him "skill to understand" (Dan. 9:20-23).

I set my face toward the Lord God to make request by prayer with fasting, sackcloth, and ashes ... While I was speaking in prayer ... Gabriel ... talked with me, and said, "O Daniel, I have now come forth to give you skill to understand ... consider the matter, and understand the vision" (Dan. 9:3, 21-23).

Then he said to me, "Do not fear, Daniel, for from the first day that you set your heart to understand, and to humble yourself before your God, your words were heard; and I have come because of your words" (Dan. 10:12).

It takes supernatural skill to understand the deeper things in God's heart and His plans for the End Times. We will not gain this understanding by natural means. It will take encounters with God. He will send angels to some of His end-time prophets like He did to Daniel. We must set our hearts to seek prophetic understanding, as Daniel did, by fasting and praying for supernatural understanding.

3. Fasting for the fulfillment of God's promises to our city or nation

The Lord has prophetic plans and promises for each city on Earth. He has given the Church in your region promises just as He has done for the Church here in Kansas City. We must not attempt to passively receive these promises with an idle faith. The Lord intends for us to actively petition Him for their fulfillment. There is no activity more integral to this than sustained corporate intercessory worship and prayer with fasting.

Scripture is full of examples of men of faith used by God to usher in the completion of His promises. For example, God had said that He would restore the Israelites from their horrible 70-year captivity as slaves in Babylon (606-536 BC). When the Persians conquered Babylon, Daniel prayed and fasted for the fulfillment of God's promises. As a result, Israel was released from captivity and allowed to return to its land and rebuild its nation (Dan. 9:1-3; 10:1-3). A few years later, Nehemiah, while still in the Persian capital of Shushan, heard reports of the terrible struggle his fellow Jews were having back home in Israel. The wall and gates of Jerusalem were still broken down; they had no protection from the surrounding enemies. Nehemiah, like Daniel, sought the Lord with fasting and prayer, asking that God would fulfill His promises to that generation in Israel. Nehemiah fasted, wept and confessed Israel's sins, and prayed for God to release His promises for Israel (Neh. 1:1-11; 9:32-38). God answered Nehemiah's prayers and blessed Israel at that time. The prophetess Anna fasted and prayed for more than 60 years that God would visit Israel and fulfill His promises to them (Luke 2:36-38). God answered by allowing her to see the infant Jesus, the long-awaited Messiah who would save Israel.

Jesus told His disciples that the harvest of souls was plentiful, and those who sowed in prayer and those who reaped in evangelism would rejoice together (John 4:34-38). In other words, the first work to be done in Israel's harvest was the labor of prayer and fasting. Thus, the labor of Jesus, Anna, Simeon, and John the Baptist paved the way for the revival the apostles reaped after the Pentecostal outpouring.

When Cornelius fasted and prayed, God sent him an angelic messenger and the apostle Peter, leading to salvation for his whole household (Acts 10:1-4, 30-31). The spirit of revival was poured out on the region and a door of grace was opened for the Gentiles. The apostle Paul embraced fasting as a key to releasing God's promises for his ministry (Acts 9:15; 26:17-18; 2 Cor. 6:5; 11:27). He also prayed and fasted for a revival spirit to touch the churches in Galatia, bringing them to spiritual maturity (Gal. 4:19).

Today, as we see multitudes headed for Hell and a Church that is spiritually barren and lacking power for healing and deliverance, our biblical response should be the same as those whose responses are recorded in the Bible. We must pray and fast until we see a breakthrough of the things that God has promised our city and nation.

4. Fasting to stop a crisis

Fasting to avert a national or individual crisis was often practiced in Old Testament times. Time after time God reversed the Israelites' desperate situation when they turned to Him in corporate prayer and fasting. In the prophet Joel's day, Israel faced several divine judgments. First, locusts and drought brought on an agricultural crisis (Joel 1). Then the Babylonian army prepared to invade the land (Joel 2:1-9). Joel called for a national solemn assembly, proclaiming that God might reverse His decision to judge them if the people humbled themselves and repented with fasting and prayer (Joel 1:13-14; 2:12-15).

The prophet Jonah was sent to warn the wicked Assyrian city of Nineveh that the God of Israel was going to destroy them. When the people of Nineveh humbled themselves and repented with fasting, the Lord showed mercy and spared the city (Jonah 3:3-9).

Moses fasted on Mount Sinai and received the Ten Commandments and directions for building the Tabernacle, but when he came down the mountain he found the people worshipping idols. God was ready to destroy Israel, but Moses immediately entered into a second 40-day fast with prayer (Deut. 9:7-21). God spared Israel because of Moses' intercession.

In the same way, Ezra the priest mourned over the compromise he found in the children of Israel. When he arrived in Jerusalem, he found they had intermarried with the pagans even though they knew this was expressly forbidden in Scripture. Correcting the problem was complex, because new families had been started and children had been born. Ezra fasted with great grief, knowing this compromise deeply displeased God and would lead to further idolatry in Israel (Ezra 9:1-6). Ezra's prayer and confession caused many others to be convicted of their sin. They gathered to confess and stop their compromise (Ezra 10:1-6). God's favor was restored to Israel and judgment was averted.

Fasting for national deliverance has been practiced throughout history. England's leaders have called national days of prayer and fasting at several notable times of crisis. In 1588 the nation fasted when it was threatened by the Spanish Armada. Later, they fasted for God's help as Napoleon prepared to invade England. Again, during World War II, George VI called a day of prayer and fasting while the Battle of Britain raged, asking God to stop the Nazis from invading. On each of these three occasions God spared England from a great crisis.

The principle of humbling oneself with fasting during a time of crisis is also seen on a personal level throughout Scripture. Hannah, the mother of Samuel, was so distressed by her physical barrenness that "she wept and did not eat." God answered her cry and lifted the crisis of her barrenness by giving her a son who grew up to become a mighty prophet (1 Sam. 1:7).

David also understood that repentance with fasting was his only hope to preserve the life of the child he'd conceived through his adulterous relationship with Bathsheba (2 Sam. 12:15-23). In this case, the Lord took the life of the child, but this situation shows that in personal crisis David knew that turning to God with prayer and fasting was his only hope (Ps. 35:13; 69:10; 109:24).

In the days of the young King Josiah, a prophetess named Huldah sent word to the king saying that God was preparing to judge Israel because of the people's sin. Josiah responded with fasting and prayer (2 Chr. 34:23-28). God saw Josiah's sincere heart and delayed the judgment of the Babylonian invasion until after Josiah's death.

King Ahab was one of the most wicked kings in Israel's history. He humbled himself with prayer and fasting and God stopped the judgment that was set against him (1 Kings 21:25-29). The same was true of King Manasseh, who was also an evil king in Israel. He humbled himself and received God's mercy, instead of the sure judgment that was to come on him (2 Chr. 33:9-13).

5. Fasting for protection

Fasting for personal protection is also scriptural. After the Jewish captives from Babylon returned to Israel to begin rebuilding their nation, they needed help. Ezra the priest led a group of people back to Israel to help them rebuild Jerusalem. While they were still making preparations to travel, they took time to fast and pray, asking God for protection on the dangerous journey. The dangers of travel in the ancient world were serious because bands of thieves attacked traveling groups and robbed them of their gold and supplies. They usually killed all the people and sold their possessions. Ezra did not want to request an escort of soldiers from the Persian king, however, for he had told the king that God's blessing would be on them. He fasted and prayed and asked God for supernatural protection as they passed through foreign lands. God answered Ezra (Ezra 8:21-23).

When Daniel was thrown into the lions' den, King Darius and Daniel fasted and prayed for Daniel's protection. In response, God sent an angel into the lions' den to shut the mouths of the lions (Dan. 6:18-23). Daniel's life was spared as a result of prayer and fasting.

Esther, a Jewish woman in the Persian court, called the Jews in Persia to fast for three days after a wicked man named Haman set into motion a plan to annihilate all the Jews and take their possessions (Esth. 3:13; 4:7). Esther first needed divine protection when she came before King Ahasuerus (Xerxes) without a royal summons. The penalty for doing what Esther did was death. Many cried out in prayer and fasting (Esth. 4:3, 16). The Lord spared Esther's life before the king (Esth. 5:1-6) and then reversed the situation facing the Jews and saved them from Haman's evil plan (Esth. 9:1).

When Peter was in prison, the early Church gathered for constant prayer. In answer, God sent an angel to Peter in the night. His chains fell off and the iron gate to the city opened of its own accord (Acts 12:1-19). Church history is filled with examples of how prayer and fasting led to the deliverance of God's servants from peril and danger. This will happen often in the End Times (Ps. 91).

6. Fasting for direction

Immediately after Paul's conversion on the road to Damascus, he fasted for three days, waiting to receive clear direction from the Lord (Acts 9:9). Throughout the New Testament, we see the Church fasting for supernatural wisdom and direction. While in Antioch, Paul and his team fasted and prayed for prophetic direction. God spoke clearly, giving them a strategic missions assignment to reach the Gentiles, as recorded in Acts 13:1-2. This missionary tour changed history. Paul and his team again prayed with fasting when they needed to select and commission the elder of the new churches in Lystra, Iconium and Antioch. "When they had appointed elders in every church, and prayed with fasting, they commended them to the Lord in whom they had believed" (Acts 14:23).

Jesus prayed all night to receive direction before selecting His twelve apostles. "He went out to the mountain to pray, and continued all night in prayer to God. And when it was day, He called His disciples to Himself; and from them He chose twelve whom He also named apostles" (Luke 6:12-13).

7. Fasting for encounter and intimacy with God – the Bridegroom fast

"The disciples of John came to Him, saying, 'Why do we and the Pharisees fast often, but Your disciples do not fast?' Jesus said to them, 'Can the friends of the bridegroom mourn as long as the bridegroom is with them? But the days will come when the

bridegroom will be taken away from them, and then they will fast'"
(Matt. 9:14-15).

During Jesus' time on Earth, the disciples grew accustomed
to His presence. They felt cherished and loved by Him and they
rejoiced in the intimacy of His friendship. Jesus said the joy they
were experiencing in His nearness would become grief and longing
when He was taken from them at His death. He spoke of a new
kind of fast based on His identity as the Bridegroom God and their
desire to be with Him. They would fast in mourning because of
His absence and fast in longing for His return. They would fast to
increase their experience of His presence and their revelation of His
beauty and affection for them. This is what we call the "Bridegroom
fast." It is primarily fueled by *desiring Jesus* rather than by a desire
for more power in ministry or escape from judgment and crisis.

A precursor to the Bridegroom fast was Yom Kippur, the Day of
Atonement, which was an annual time of fasting for Israel to mourn
over their sin and seek renewal (Lev. 23:26-32). God established
this fast by divine revelation (Lev. 16:29), whereas other fasts in
the Jewish calendar, such as Purim, and that which is described in
Zechariah 7 and 8, find their origins in historic tradition. Paul and his
companions may have observed the Day of Atonement fast during
his journey to Rome (Acts 27:9).

God has promised to reveal the depths of His heart to us (1
Cor. 2:10). Just a small taste of His love makes us insatiably hungry
for more, and fasting accelerates the rate at which we receive
revelation from God. As we enter into a Bridegroom fast, our sins
are mourned, our hearts are stirred with longing for Jesus, and our
spiritual capacity to freely receive from Him is increased.

Fasting for intimacy and for spiritual renewal also includes
mourning over the sin that hinders our relationship with Him. We
mourn out of our desire to be one with God and over our unlikeness
to Him. We feel the pain of our immaturity and all the things we have
harbored in our lives that stand in the way of our intimacy with God.
This is a godly sorrow and is one of the ways the Lord brings us into

alignment with Himself. David spoke of humbling and cleansing his soul with fasting as he confronted the sins that hindered his ability to behold the beauty of God (Ps. 27:4; 35:13; 69:10; 109:24). This mourning is meant to "afflict" our souls (Is. 58:3, 5), as we renounce everything that sets itself up against the knowledge of God's love in our lives.

A Few Practical Details About Fasting

Various Lengths of Fasts Described in the Bible

◆ One-day fast as on the Day of Atonement (Lev. 16:29; 23:27).

◆ Three-day fast as embraced by Paul after his conversion (Acts 9:9).

◆ Seven-day fast as done by David before his child died (2 Sam. 12:15-18, 21-23).

◆ Three-week fast as done by Daniel seeking to understand prophetic Scriptures (Dan. 10:2, 3).

◆ Forty-day fast as done by Moses (Ex. 24:18; 34:28; Deut. 9:9, 18); Elijah (1 Kin. 19:8); and Jesus during His temptation (Matt. 4:2-3).

Biblical Examples of Corporate Fasting

◆ The Church fasted and prayed for Peter's deliverance from prison (Acts 12:1-19).

◆ Paul and his team in Antioch fasted to receive prophetic direction (Act 13:1-3).

◆ Paul and his team fasted as they commissioned elders in Lystra, Iconium and Antioch (Acts 14:23).

◆ Israel fasted on Yom Kippur or the Day of Atonement (Lev. 16:29; 23:37; Acts 27:9).

◆ Israel fasted during Purim (Esth. 9:30-31).

◆ Israel fasted in the fourth, fifth, seventh and tenth months during captivity (Zech 7:3-5; 8:19).

- Israel fasted at Mizpah before the Philistines attacked (1 Sam. 7:3-10).
- Israel fasted when at civil war with the Benjaminites (Judg. 20:26-28).
- Jehoshaphat and Israel fasted before going to war with Moab and Ammon (2 Chr. 20:3-4).
- King Josiah humbled himself (2 Kin. 22:11-20).
- The people of Israel fasted in King Jehoiakim's day (Jer. 36:9-10).
- Joel's call to national solemn assemblies (Joel 1:13-14; 2:12-15).
- Esther and Israel fasted before a coming holocaust in Persia (Esth. 3:13; 4:3, 7, 16; 5:6).
- Ezra and others fasted to seek God for protection on the way to Jerusalem (Ezra 8:21-23).
- Nehemiah and Israel in Jerusalem fasted for spiritual renewal (Neh. 9:1).
- Nineveh fasted after Jonah's preaching (Jonah 3:3-9).

Biblical Examples of Individual Fasting

- Believers fast to experience Jesus as the Bridegroom God (Matt. 9:14-15).
- Jesus fasted for 40 days (Matt. 4:1-3; Luke 4:1-2).
- Moses fasted on Mount Sinai for 40 days (Ex. 24:18; 34:28; Deut. 9:9, 18).
- Elijah fasted for 40 days on the way to Mt. Horeb/Sinai (1 Kin. 19:8).
- John the Baptist led a fasted lifestyle (Matt. 11:18).
- Paul led a fasted lifestyle (2 Cor. 6:5; 11:27; Gal. 4:19).
- Paul fasted for three days to receive clear direction (Acts 9:9).
- Paul fasted to receive clear direction in ministry situations (Acts 13:1-2; 14:23).

- Daniel fasted to receive revelation about the End Times (Dan. 9:1-3, 20-23; 10:1-3, 12-14).
- King Darius fasted all night for Daniel's protection in the lions' den (Dan. 6:18-23).
- Anna the prophetess lived a lifestyle of fasting and prayer for more than 60 years (Luke 2:36-37).
- Cornelius prayed and fasted for spiritual breakthrough (Acts 10:1-4, 30-31).
- Esther fasted for Israel's deliverance (Esth. 4:16-5:6).
- King Ahab humbled himself with prayer and fasting (1 Kin. 21:25-29).
- Hannah fasted over her barrenness (1 Sam. 1:7-8).
- David fasted often (2 Sam. 12:15-23; Ps. 35:13; 69:10; 109:24).
- Ezra fasted as he mourned over Israel's intermarriages with pagans (Ezra 9:1-6).
- Ezra fasted again as the people joined him in repentance (Ezra 10:1-6).
- Nehemiah fasted in Jerusalem for Israel's spiritual renewal (Neh. 9:1).
- Nehemiah fasted for Israel's restoration (Neh. 1:1-11) and renewal (Neh 9:32-38).

CHAPTER THREE

Understanding the Bridegroom Fast

The disciples of John came to Him, saying, "Why do we and the Pharisees fast often, but Your disciples do not fast?" Jesus said to them, "Can the friends of the bridegroom mourn as long as the bridegroom is with them? But the days will come when the bridegroom will be taken away from them, and then they will fast. No one puts a piece of unshrunk cloth on an old garment; for the patch pulls away from the garment, and the tear is made worse. Nor do they put new wine into old wineskins, or else the wineskins break, the wine is spilled, and the wineskins are ruined. But they put new wine into new wineskins, and both are preserved" (Matt. 9:14-17).

A New Covenant Fast

John the Baptist's disciples came to Jesus with a zealous and sincere question. They were confused and troubled by the lack of fasting among His disciples. John had taught his own disciples to fast often, and they saw that even the hypocritical Pharisees recognized how essential the discipline was. Did Jesus not value fasting? Did

He lack the discipleship and leadership skills to teach it to His men? John's disciples' intense hunger for God had led them to give up everything in their pursuit of Him. The implication behind their question was that John was a more spiritual leader than Jesus.

Jesus answered their question by asking them what seemed a strange question. "Can the friends of the bridegroom mourn as long as the bridegroom is with them?" He then made another unusual statement, saying the days were coming when the Bridegroom would be taken from them. He was referring to Himself as the Bridegroom who would be taken from them by dying on the cross. He implied that then His disciples would fast with the same consistency and intensity that John's disciples did. Their fasting, however, would flow out of longing and mourning for Jesus as a Bridegroom. Jesus used their question to introduce Himself as a Bridegroom this was His first reference in Scripture to being the Bridegroom. He was introducing a new paradigm of fasting—a fast motivated by desire to encounter His beautiful and loving presence.

In the Old Testament, fasting was usually an expression of sorrow over sin or a plea for God to physically deliver His people from disaster. In many cases it had degenerated into a purely religious exercise, as the legalistic Pharisees practiced. Now the Lord was saying there was something new. After His death, after the New Covenant had been established, fasting would take on a whole new dimension. The indwelling Holy Spirit in each believer would make this possible. The fast His disciples would enter into would be one related to intimacy with Jesus as the Bridegroom.

In the New Covenant, God opened the depths of His heart to every believer through the Holy Spirit (1 Cor. 2:10; Heb. 10:19-22). It is a privilege beyond comprehension that weak humans can experience the depths of God's heart. This is our inheritance and our destiny. We must never be content to live without a growing experience of God's heart. "For the Spirit searches all things, yes, the deep things of God ... We have received ... the Spirit that we might know the things ... freely given to us by God" (1 Cor. 2:10-12).

The apostles experienced this intimacy of knowing the Man Christ Jesus while He walked the Earth. Jesus insisted they not fast during this time, but rejoice. Just as there will be no fasting in the age to come because we will be face to face with Him, it would have been unnecessary for the disciples to fast when God was their daily companion.

But things changed for the apostles after Jesus was taken away by death. The promise of the New Covenant was still theirs— intimacy with Jesus—but His physical presence was gone. They mourned and longed to experience more of His presence. He had awakened a depth of desire in their hearts that they were not fully aware of until they were wounded by His absence. They longed for Him, for His nearness. When the overflowing gladness of His immediate presence was taken from them, they were heartsick. Then they fasted.

The Bridegroom Fast is About Desire

Song of Solomon 5:8 says, "If you find my Beloved ... tell him I am lovesick!" The Song of Solomon describes the relationship between Jesus, the Bridegroom, and the Church, His Bride. It describes the Church's lovesickness for God (Song 2:5; 5:8). Even the remembrance of our close encounters with Jesus in years past create a hunger today, a craving that will not be satisfied until we experience Him again and again in even greater measures. Lovesickness is mourning for the loving presence of Jesus as the Bridegroom God. No one can console our lovesick hearts except Him. A heart that does not mourn for more of Him is a heart that accepts its current state of spiritual barrenness as tolerable and livable. A mourning heart is fiercely discontent; it has a desperate hunger for God. This is the Bridegroom fast.

The Bridegroom fast is focused on desire: both understanding God's desire for us and awakening our own desire for Him. God imparts new desires to us as He answers existent ones. The hope of a lovesick heart will not be disappointed, for Jesus promised that we would be satisfied as we mourn for more of Him. "Blessed are those who mourn, for they shall be comforted" (Matt. 5:4). "Blessed are those who hunger and thirst for righteousness, for they shall be filled" (Matt. 5:6).

The joy that the early apostles experienced in Jesus' nearness became grief and longing, even lovesickness, when Jesus was taken from them. This same longing and lovesickness has a dynamic purpose in us. Spiritual hunger is a divine gift that leads us to seek greater experiences of His love, regardless of the cost. It causes us to be willing to make whatever changes are necessary in our hearts and lives in order for love to have its way.

We were made to love and be loved by God and He has made us to crave Him until our heart cry is answered. He increases our experience of Him by awakening and then answering desire within us. First, in the initial stages, He romances us, lets us feel His love stir within us. Though this brings a certain satisfaction to our souls, it also awakens a deeper longing and hunger for more. Once we taste just a little of God's presence, we cannot live without more of Him. This is the way God planned it. Hunger begets hunger and deep calls unto deep (Ps. 42:7). In every satisfaction God brings to us, we are left with an even greater hunger for more of Him. It is by our hunger that He leads us into the fullness of love. We fast in response to the groan in our hearts for more of God.

The Purpose of the Bridegroom Fast

Why would Jesus want His friends to mourn while He was away? Isn't He a God of joy who wants His followers to live lives characterized by that same joy? These questions bring us to the heart of the Bridegroom fast and its purpose. Yes, we were made to live in joy, but that joy can be found only in the Person and presence of Jesus. Joy apart from Jesus is no joy at all.

Mourning and fasting for the Bridegroom is our way of positioning our hearts to live by desire for God and not by the lusts of this age. Our mourning for Him gives witness that we are not of this world and that we refuse to come under the seductions of

Satan, the ruler of this world. This holy longing will not ultimately or fully be satisfied until we live face to face with Jesus in the age to come. His second coming is ultimately the fullness of the answer and consolation for which we mourn. It is in His coming that our highest joy will be found (Ps. 119:19,20; Rom. 8:23-25; Heb. 11:16). Until that day, however, we will continue to groan within ourselves, eagerly waiting for Him to come once again.

The purpose of the Bridegroom fast goes even beyond yearning for Jesus' return—it is the yearning to experience His presence now. In the midst of the delay, the waiting between His first and second coming, God allows us to experience a measure of His presence. He has sent the Holy Spirit so we can encounter His presence and love in measure even now. The Bridegroom fast enlarges our hearts to experience that divine love and presence now.

God has designed us so that when we give ourselves to Him by fasting and reading the Word, our capacity to receive more of Him increases. No other dimension in the grace of God opens wide the deepest places of our beings like fasting and filling our hearts with the Scriptures that emphasize the truths of Jesus as our Bridegroom. Fasting serves as a catalyst to increase the *depth* and the *measure* to which we receive from the Lord. By fasting we receive *greater measures* of revelation at an *accelerated pace*, which has a *deeper impact* upon our hearts.

One of the primary purposes of the Bridegroom fast is to cause our hearts to move in love and longing for God. We do not fast in an attempt to make God pay attention to us, but to fully enter into the affection and presence of God that is already ours in Christ. It is not to move His heart but to move our own. Our hearts are prone to dullness and lethargy, and if we don't deliberately confront that dullness, we become hardened without realizing it. The Bridegroom fast tenderizes our hearts so dullness is diminished and we are able to experience the affections of God in greater measure. Our hearts become tender and our desire is nurtured as we experience the pleasures of knowing Him.

I emphasize that our desire for God is His gift to us. However, this craving for God causes pain in our hearts. We are wounded in love. This works good things in us. He does not inflict meaningless heartache upon us, so we can be sure that this longing has a purpose. Spiritual hunger is a divine agent that leads us to greater love. It is an instrument that makes room for love and purity in our hearts and expands our souls. We cannot enter into the fullness of love without the preparatory impact of mourning for more of Him.

Our desire for Jesus creates the mourning or the pain of lovesickness, which in turn compels us to make changes in our lives so that we can receive all that is ours in God. We are wounded in love because He intentionally withholds a measure of His presence in order to bring us into greater intimacy as He works humility and produces meekness in us so God's nearness is sustained in us for the long term.

The Bridegroom fast also brings holiness to our souls. Fasting for spiritual renewal includes mourning over the sin that hinders our relationship with Him. The increase of lovesickness for God inevitably causes a conviction within and we become unable to tolerate anything that opposes the life of God in us. No longer are we content to live in compromise or sin—we surrender everything because lovesickness compels us. Fasting is meant to "afflict" our souls as we renounce everything that sets itself up against the knowledge of God's love and power in our lives (Is. 58:3, 5). David spoke of humbling and chastening his soul with fasting as he confronted the sins that hindered his ability to behold the beauty of God (Ps. 27:4; 35:13; 69:10; 109:24).

Fasting because of love exposes the compromises in our hearts and our ungodly dependence on worldly things. It is a way of keeping our hearts spiritually awake and alert in a dark world that naturally dulls and defiles the human spirit. Our love for God must be expressed in our quest to pursue total obedience. Jesus said, "He who has My commandments and keeps them, it is he who loves Me. And he who loves Me will be loved by My Father, and I will love him and manifest Myself to him" (John 14:21).

One key way to sustain our love in God as we seek to live righteously, is to wage war with the lusts inside us. Lust has many different expressions, including pride, anger, covetousness, theft, immorality, pornography, bitterness, hatred, slander, jealousy, drunkenness, over-indulgence with food or entertainment, legal and illegal addictions, and others (Mark 7:21-22; Gal. 5:19-21; 1 John 2:16-17). 1 Peter 2:11 says, "Beloved, I beg you as sojourners and pilgrims, abstain from fleshly lusts which war against the soul." So, mourning for the Bridegroom also involves repentance. To mourn is to rend or to tear our hearts, as the prophet Joel insisted: "Turn to Me with all your heart, with fasting, with weeping, and with mourning. So rend your heart ... for He is gracious and merciful ..." (Joel 2:12-13). As we fast with hearts tender toward the Lord, we are kept in the position of continually rending our hearts and inviting the Holy Spirit to search us, to see if there is any wicked way in us (Ps. 139:23-24). Fasting is a God-given gift that helps us "break out" of the cares of this life and the corruption of sin and darkness. It enables us to get free from the grip of our culture's seductions that we might lay hold of the purpose for which God laid hold of us (Phil. 3:12).

A High Vision is Necessary in Fasting

Anyone who desires to live a life characterized by fasting must begin with a high vision, a vision to experience the fullness of what God wants to give each of us in this age. We fast because we cannot endure living in spiritual barrenness. The person who fasts understands the gap between what God wants to give them and what they are actually experiencing. The lack in our experience causes us to be discontent and to mourn. When we recognize that there is a realm in God to which we are invited but not yet experiencing, we become ruined. We must have this fullness. This state of "ruinedness" is an essential part of the lifestyle of fasting. Without a vision or hope for attaining more in God, we will not fast.

The Church today needs a renewed vision of fasting. We need to recognize it as a gift from God that leads the human spirit into fascination and exhilaration before Him. God has given us the grace of the Bridegroom fast that we might maximize the privilege of encountering the Bridegroom God, Jesus. Fasting is not intended by God to be something we hate. It is a gift meant to tenderize our hearts and bring great change in our lives. Fasting expresses our vision and determination to have more of God, and the pain of recognizing the ways in which we fall short. We fast because we believe God desires to take the vision He has marked us with and bring it to fruition over time. We believe in Jesus' promise that there truly are rewards given by His Father, and we refuse to live as though this promise were not true (Matt. 6:17, 18).

New Wine and New Wineskins

No one puts a piece of unshrunk cloth on an old garment; for the patch pulls away from the garment, and the tear is made worse. Nor do they put new wine into old wineskins, or else the wineskins break, the wine is spilled, and the wineskins are ruined. But they put new wine into new wineskins, and both are preserved (Matt. 9:16-17).

Immediately after Jesus introduced the idea of the Bridegroom fast, He spoke of new wine being placed into new wineskins (Matt. 9:16-17). It is notable that He prophesied of new wineskins in the context of the Bridegroom fast. New wine speaks of the presence of the Holy Spirit and His impact on people as He releases power in us that causes us to rejoice in love. His wine is always "new," for He continually imparts new and fresh revelation about God's heart. It is not that the Scriptures are new, but that the discovery of or emphasis on certain Scriptures is new to a particular generation.

Right now, the Spirit is raising up many men and women who are having and will have new and fresh encounters with Jesus. They are the old treasures that the saints over the ages have experienced, yet they are new to us. The end result will be an anointed company of people who have fascinated and lovesick hearts for Jesus. But where does such a company of believers fit in with the current culture of spiritual compromise in the Church?

New Wineskins

New wineskins represent the new structures necessary to serve the people who have new wine experiences. The people of the new wine see God, themselves and their missions very differently than they did before they encountered Jesus as a Bridegroom. They have new values and new paradigms of the Kingdom. These newly lovesick believers need new structures, and these new structures must be governed by leaders who share the values that flow from experiencing the Bridegroom's affections and power. Those with the old wineskin paradigms, values and control cannot lead such people.

Jesus spoke of new wineskins for that generation, pointing to the new structures that would come forth as a result of the outpouring of the Spirit on the day of Pentecost. He knew the synagogue system would not be sufficient to provide structure for those who were continually experiencing His power, revelation and passion. Jesus was prophesying that the old structures would break and the wine would spill out and be lost. The Lord soon replaced the existing old wineskin (the religious synagogue structure) with a New Testament community of believers led by unlikely people, such as fishermen, ex-prostitutes and tax collectors. This principle of needing new wineskins for a new move of the Spirit has been repeated many times through history, and will be repeated again at the end of the age.

Today, the Holy Spirit again desires to pour out new wine—the active presence of the Bridegroom. God will give us everything He gave the early Church. In the generation in which the Lord returns, the miracles of the Book of Acts will be combined with the miracles of the Book of Exodus. When the Holy Spirit comes in full manifest power, whatever wineskins do not agree with Him will be ruined and broken. It's not possible to dwell with God except in unity with Him. The Holy Spirit wine will only be continually poured out into an environment or structure that is suited to Him. The wine of the newly emphasized truths the Holy Spirit highlights in a revival are often lost in old systems. Nothing is more tragic than the wine being spilled and the Spirit's manifest presence and power leaving. Some old structures in this day will be revived and renewed. However, most will not. History shows that a new move of God is resisted by people. Great changes are coming in our experiences, as well as with our Church and ministry structures.

In the coming hour, untold millions will experience new dimensions of God's heart and power as they encounter Him as the Bridegroom King and Judge. The religious structures of today are predominantly led by those who are not lovesick. They will not know what to do with ex-prostitutes and fishermen who are anointed with lovesickness. The Bridegroom fast is one of the vehicles through which this wave of lovesickness will overtake the Church, resulting in the creation of new structures to accommodate them. The revelation of Jesus as the Bridegroom, along with the Bridegroom fast, will be a vital part of transitioning from the old wineskin systems to New Testament Church structures and way of life.

CHAPTER FOUR

Hungering For All That God Will Give Us

(Dana speaking) I remember several years ago when the Lord really began convicting my heart of how little hunger I had for God. He opened my understanding to how much He truly wanted to give me and showed me the gap between that fullness and my actual experience. He began to purposely disrupt my life by revealing to me the principle that He gives more of Himself in accordance with my hunger for more. Until my capacity to receive from Him was enlarged by spiritual hunger, I would be limited in my experience of God.

Though I'd known Jesus my whole life, I had never considered that I lacked this inward hunger. My heart was very small in its capacity, but I did not know it. I thought I loved God intensely, but He revealed to me that, in truth, my thirst for Him was small compared with what it could be. This exposure was truly a gift. At that time I entered into what I now call "the longing to long" or "the hungering to hunger." I was in the tension between sincerely *wanting to want* God and not yet being overcome by hunger for Him; and this is exactly where God wanted me. Hunger begets hunger and in time, He caused my initial desire to develop into strong desire, and then

He answered me with more of Himself, just as He loves to do. Jesus said, "Blessed are those who hunger and thirst for righteousness, for they shall be filled" (Matt. 5:6).

Jesus releases His power and presence to us in direct proportion to the measure of our hunger for Him. Spiritual hunger comes as we get a vision to have everything that God will give our spirit on this side of eternity. God wants to take believers beyond even what the early Christians experienced in the Book of Acts. Before He returns, He will pour out the Holy Spirit in degrees that the Church historically has never witnessed. The utter vastness of what He wants to flood our beings with in terms of experience of divine pleasure and power encounters with the Holy Spirit, has not yet even entered our minds (1 Cor. 2:9-12). Yet this fullness, this abundance of divine reward imparted to the inner man, is what God wants to give us a vision to pursue. Again, He will give according to our hunger; thus, our first priority must be to become hungry.

Some think they are spiritually hungry when they have a newly awakened interest in the things of God. But awakened interest is not yet hunger. Buying a book on a Kingdom topic is good, but it is not yet hunger. Hunger is when we cannot live without more, when we make radical alterations to our lifestyles in order to pursue God. A good way to measure the reality of our hunger is to measure the extent to which we rearrange our lives, our time, our money and our comforts to pursue that for which we hunger.

Jeremiah prophesied about genuine spiritual hunger when the Lord spoke these words through him, "You will call upon Me and go and pray to Me, and I will listen to you. And you will seek Me and find Me, when you search for Me with all your heart. I will be found by you, says the Lord" (Jer. 29:12-14). God promises that He will be found when He is pursued by anyone with a genuinely hungry heart.

Jeremiah taught us that just saying prayers is not what God requires. Spiritual language and grandiose statements in prayer do not impress God. He peers right into the depths of the human heart and sees our spiritual void and barrenness. This is where much of the Church in the western world misses the mark. We may regularly attend church services and may even go to a few prayer meetings. We may tell God that we love Him and want more in our relationship with Him. Yet all the while God is calling us to live the radically different lifestyle necessary for us to experience deep intimacy with Him. He is after something far deeper than regular attendance at prayer meetings. He wants to actually *possess* us. He wants our lives to be governed and ruled by our yearning for Him. Spiritual hunger is of utmost importance to our sustained pursuit of God.

We need more personal encounters with God, but we also hunger for His power to be released in signs and wonders and miracles. The manifestation of His power is also preceded by a desperate hunger. The Church must operate in sustained, intense prayer, coupled with fasting, in order for God's manifest power to break out in our midst. As long as we are content with paralytics not walking, the blind not seeing and the deaf not hearing, we will go without these miracles. The breakthrough we long for will not happen without spiritual intensity (Jer. 29:13), so in His grace the Lord is making us a people who cannot live without His full blessing. Our part is to become so ruined by the high vision of all that God would give us, that we simply cannot live with things as they are. We must do our part and God will do His.

Spiritual Violence

In the Old Testament there was a great limitation on what a believer could experience in God. The door for *all* to enter the deep things of the Spirit (1 Cor. 2:10) was only opened when Jesus established the New Covenant by His death, resurrection and giving of the Holy Spirit to the hearts of men (Heb. 10:19-22). Before this, the Spirit of God would occasionally come on certain people—usually prophets or kings—to anoint them to accomplish a specific task. However, after the death and resurrection of Jesus, the Holy Spirit was made accessible to all. He now indwells and empowers every believer, giving experiential nearness to all who are hungry for His presence. This is a massive transition, a gift and invitation so boundless and glorious, I do not think that we have really fathomed what has taken place. He has made everything available to us by His Holy Spirit in our inner man! The weight of this gift is so great that it should leave us trembling in awe.

Jesus opened a whole new understanding of how to live life in the Spirit when he taught that the Kingdom of God suffers violence, or allows spiritual violence to be employed. "From the days of John the Baptist until now, the kingdom of heaven suffers violence, and the violent take it by force" (Matt. 11:12). For the Kingdom to "suffer" violence means that it "permits" (rewards or requires) spiritual violence in our pursuit of God. Yes, everything is available to us in the Spirit, but we must actively walk into it. We must lay hold of it. In this passage, Jesus invited us to spiritual violence saying in essence, "The Kingdom of Heaven allows for violence—will anyone receive this invitation?" This applies to more than the obvious areas of spiritual warfare. He was urging us to pursue deep intimacy with Him with a holy, violent love and to cultivate a lifestyle of "spiritual violence."

Once again, fasting plays a vital and irreplaceable role. It is "violent" in both its demands and its impact on our lives. It demands that we address every area in our life that is not in agreement with the Spirit. It requires that we declare war against sin and Satan and against a religious spirit. However, it releases a gloriously violent impact on our lives by freeing us from our sinful ways and filling us with the revelation of God.

To be spiritually violent means we will pay any price of self-denial in order to obey God's will. Solomon said it well: "If a man would give for love all the wealth of his house, it would be utterly despised" (Song 8:7). In other words, when love is working its way in our hearts, there is no price too high. For the one he loves, a man would give all his possessions freely without consideration of the cost. The source of our spiritual violence is not fear; it is the love of

God. Any type of violence or abandonment that is not rooted in love is what Paul described as profiting nothing (1 Cor. 13:3). Love fuels our spiritual intensity.

Radical obedience is disruptive to our flesh, but it causes our spirit to soar in God. It confronts and reorders the way we spend time and money, the way we talk and entertain ourselves, and the way we express our sexuality and pursue success or honor. It is not a casual reality. It touches every area of our lives. Fasting is as violent in its opposition to our own flesh and pride as it is in its impact on the devil's kingdom and religious systems. Yet on the inside, we begin to touch what we were made for as strongholds are broken and we are freed to soar in God.

Jesus connected spiritual violence to the radical lifestyle of John the Baptist. He called John the greatest man born of a woman (Matt. 11:11). What was the measure of John's greatness? What was it that Jesus referenced in this marvelous description of John? Assuredly, it was not the size of his ministry or the number of people he impacted. The numbers were very low compared to the sizes of mega ministries that are common today. Jesus was referring to John's spiritual violence. John carried a tremendous resolve to follow God without compromise and thus Jesus described him with such a strong acclamation.

We too can be great in God if we are resolute, violent, in our obedience to Him. Can you imagine standing before the throne of God one day and hearing the actual voice of Jesus, that Voice of many waters, declare, "I call you great in My sight"? Greatness to God is about love, obedience and meekness—it is about a violent resolve in the heart of those who seek Him. Whoever wants to be great in God *may*. The Kingdom of Heaven allows for violence, and the violent take it by force.

Pursuing the Full Measure

"Take heed what you hear. With the same measure you use, it will be measured to you; and to you who hear, more will be given"

(Mark 4:24). Jesus taught us to take heed what we hear—what we understand and receive as God's standard for our lives. What do we believe is the level of intimacy God is willing to draw us into? Do we really believe in the rewards that God has promised to those who align their lives in the way prescribed by His Word? Have we heard His invitation? What are we buying into as our life vision in God? What is the vision that you have for where your heart can go in God in this life?

This may surprise us, but we ourselves actually determine some of the measure of spiritual blessing He will give us, as well as some of the measure of our greatness in the age to come. Believing for too small a measure will lead to just that. Those who have truly *heard* will believe and act on what God said. To those who "hear" what God really wants to give them, more will be given. The necessary posture is that of a hearer; it is a posture of receiving His promises as true and ordering our lives so as to reach for them. What will we contend for in our experience with Him? What will we claim as our inheritance? We need to have a vision for what God will give our hearts, as well as a vision for what He will do through us in our ministry.

Do not limit your vision to just your ministry, though. We must have a vision for how far God will take our hearts in love, meekness and revelation. We must not be too easily satisfied with a small measure, for Jesus will give to us according to the measure we build our lives around. The extent of our expectation, or faith, defines what we tenaciously pursue in God. If we absolutely refuse to settle for anything less than His fullness, we will be rewarded with our desire.

Paying the Price

Most Christians do not mind hearing sermons on holiness and radical obedience. What disturbs the western Church is watching someone actually live out these principles in real-life arenas that affect their time and money. That hits too close to home. It convicts believers who haven't yet decided to live in 100-percent obedience. The reason is an automatic feeling of judgment.

Yes, God rewards spiritual violence. He will open up to us as much as we will press in for. But there is a cost. The price of obedience is not nebulous; it is not something we can simply talk about. This is where the tension begins to build. We must lay aside compromise, selfish comforts, pride, fear and religious reasoning. Obedience must be walked out in the practical issues of real life. For those of us whose souls just love being radical, here is a caution: this is not an invitation to be irresponsible. We do not need to abandon our God-given responsibilities in order to obey God. That is a contradiction. What we're talking about is a self-denying commitment to hear and obey, no matter what He tells us to do.

King David lived a life of radical obedience and consuming zeal, and it cost him the respect of many people, including his family. Psalm 69 is a Messianic psalm, which means it expresses David's life and prayer and at the same time points to Jesus our Messiah. David speaks of bearing reproach because of His zeal for God (v. 7). He was mocked for radically pursuing God. He felt like a "stranger to his brothers" (v. 8). His friends and family did not recognize him anymore because his values, his practices, and his lifestyle (v. 9) were so different from theirs. Zeal for God had consumed him, and they rejected him because of it. "Because for Your sake I have borne reproach ... I have become a stranger to my brothers ... Because zeal for Your house has eaten me up, and the reproaches of those who reproach You have fallen on me. When I wept and chastened my soul with fasting, that became my reproach. ... I became a byword to them. Those who sit in the gate speak against me, and I am the song of the drunkards" (Ps. 69:7-12).

David became like a different person from their point of view. Those close to him did not understand him anymore. He had been so changed that his friends lamented the loss of who he used to be. David was willing to bear reproach, to look foolish. In his zeal he wept and fasted. This brought even more reproach on him (v. 10).

Fasting tenderizes our spirit. The tears associated with fasting are not just tears of repentance, but also tears of tenderness. David's family didn't like him fasting and they didn't like his tears. The whole thing bothered those around him (v. 11).

At such a time as this—yes, today—God is raising up those who will pursue Him in spiritual violence, as John the Baptist did, and with the passionate zeal King David had. We do this by living a fasted lifestyle. In the following chapters, we will address why God wants us to lead a lifestyle of fasting.

CHAPTER FIVE

Fasting: Embracing Voluntary Weakness

A thorn in the flesh was given to me, a messenger of Satan to buffet me, lest I be exalted above measure. Concerning this thing I pleaded with the Lord three times that it might depart from me. He said to me, "My grace is sufficient for you, for My strength is made perfect in weakness." Therefore most gladly I will rather boast in my infirmities, that the power of Christ may rest upon me (2 Cor. 12:7-9).

*Three times I was beaten with rods; once I was stoned; three times I was shipwrecked; a night and a day I have been in the deep; ... in perils among false brethren; in weariness and toil, in sleeplessness often, in hunger and thirst, **in fastings often,** in cold and nakedness (2 Cor. 11:25-27).*

Fasting is a call to voluntarily embrace weakness in order to experience more of God's power and presence. Perhaps nothing is less appealing to us than weakness. Thus, nothing seems less inviting than embracing that weakness voluntarily. However, this is the invitation God gives us. It is a paradox that we become weak in the natural in order to receive strength from the Spirit. Why did God choose fasting as such an important way to meet Him? Why has

He made something so simple—such as praying and not eating—
so powerful? Our natural minds cannot make sense of it because
by nature we despise weakness and reject all forms of deficiency.
We love to feel strong and powerful and we despise feelings of
vulnerability and feebleness. But there is something in the realm of
weakness that God will not let us avoid.

Jesus' incarnation makes it clear that weakness is an integral part
of God's plan to bring people to Himself in love. As we think about
Jesus' life, we realize that God Himself put on the weak flesh of man
and willingly embraced physical weaknesses when He walked on
Earth. "For we do not have a High Priest who cannot sympathize with
our weaknesses, but was in all points tempted as we are, yet without
sin" (Heb. 4:15). We can call Him brother because He became as one
of us, subjecting Himself to the same weakness that we experience.
This was not an accident, but the perfect plan of God.

When Paul was struggling with God's call to walk in weakness,
Jesus encouraged him by revealing that the release of God's
power in his life was connected to his willingness to embrace
weakness (2 Cor. 12:9). This is a stunning revelation, foundational
to understanding the purpose of fasting. The weaknesses Paul
talks about in the passages above (2 Cor. 11-12) were not moral,
but results of his godly choices. They fall into two categories. First,
we see weaknesses in Paul's life that were voluntary. These include
prayer, fasting, living simply and serving with humility and diligence.
Second, there were weaknesses in Paul's ministry that were
involuntary, including the thorn in his flesh, persecution, infirmity,
reproach and distress. When Paul boasted of his weakness (2
Cor. 12:9), he was referring to both the involuntary weakness of
persecution and the voluntary weakness of the fasted lifestyle.

The Paradox of Power and Weakness

What is this "strength made perfect," this perfected power that
Paul experienced in his weaknesses? It is the greater dimensions
of God's own power. Many desire to walk in perfected power, but

do not want to embrace the weakness that is necessary to enter into it. Western culture hates weakness. We disdain the thought of becoming weak. However, weakness is mandatory for those who desire spiritual strength. Paul taught that "God has chosen the weak things of the world to put to shame the things which are mighty ... that no flesh should glory in God's presence" (1 Cor. 1:27, 29). God reveals Himself the most when we are at our weakest. Paul went so far as to boast, even rejoice, in the persecution he suffered. This has perplexed many. His reasoning, though, is simple. He had a divine revelation that weakness was the doorway into God's power, and must therefore not be avoided. Paul wanted to see God's power in his life, and understood that the surest way to experience It was in his own weaknesses, both the voluntary and involuntary ones.

There are paradoxes in the way God runs His Kingdom. He never seems to do things the way our natural wisdom would imagine. One of these paradoxes is that He releases spiritual power in answer to our physical weakness. Fasting Is not primarily a call to hunger. The most challenging issue in fasting is the physical weakness it produces, not the hunger. We become physically weak and thus can't function in the way we usually do. Our thinking is blurry, our movement is wobbly, our communication is feeble and our memory is foggy. Even the great warrior David gave testimony to being physically weak when fasting (Ps. 109:24). Both Paul and David embraced the voluntary weaknesses of the fasted lifestyle; they voluntarily subjected themselves to the vulnerabilities and difficulties of fasting and prayer. Like Paul and David, we have the choice to either embrace or neglect these weaknesses. Let us embrace them, leave behind our own strength, and forge ahead with the power that only God Himself supplies.

Fasting Reveals and Silences the Flesh

One of the first things we will encounter as we give ourselves to fasting and prayer, and the silencing of our flesh, is that our inner clanging is louder than we imagined. Nothing reveals just how noisy all of our wants and cravings are until they are denied. Those of us in Western culture, and, sadly, in the western Church, seek to immediately satisfy our natural cravings. Even Christians are deceived into seeing this as a virtue rather than as what it is, a life held captive by the domination of lust. When the inward clamoring arises, we quickly do whatever is necessary to stop the noise and silence the cravings so that we can get back to business as usual in our lives. Fasting both reveals and silences the roar and cravings of our natural man. Our flesh has a natural dominance over our spirit. Fasting is a temporary way to purposely reverse this dominance, so that our spirit man gains the upper hand for a brief time.

Scripture teaches on the necessity of denying oneself—taking up our cross to follow Jesus (Matt. 16:24). "Feeling good" and propping up our flesh with the comforts of this life is not the goal of the people of the Kingdom. Fasting is diametrically opposed to our "feel good" culture—it brings an abrupt awakening to just how much we rely upon these false and lesser comforts. The basic fact is, when I am hungry, my body does not feel good. And when I don't feel good, but can't alleviate that with food, friends and fun, the turmoil of my soul is unmasked.

We, and the Christian culture in which we live, are under the delusion that we are mightily abandoned to God, but in truth most of us are spiritually stifled and dull without knowing it. A life of fasting exposes the true reality of our spiritual health by setting us down right in the torrent of our screaming souls. And what is our real state? We cling to false pleasures and securities. We have small capacities to hear from God. We crave the approval of man. We defend our reputations. We satisfy our souls with entertainment, music and television. We are complacent and distant in our prayers. We submit to our own judgment before submitting to those in authority. We rely on outside stimulants to calm our lives. The list goes on and on. The nature of fasting and prayer is that it separates us from all the "background noise" that has been concealing these realities. In this new silence, we are forced to confront the addictions and spiritual dullness of which we've been unaware.

Nobody likes their darkness revealed and their addictions exposed. In our natural man, we would live the rest of our lives propped up by stimulants other than God and His Word. This is why the role of *desire*, that precious gift from God, is so necessary in fasting. It takes a great dissatisfaction with our current state of affairs to make us voluntarily position ourselves before God in prayer, fasting and utter vulnerability, and allow His Holy Spirit to expose the false clingings and ungodly attractions within. Only a deep craving for intimacy with God could convince us to willingly undergo the pain that accompanies this revealing of our flesh. Yet we are willing, for we know that we will only genuinely know His heart when our souls are freed from all secondary lovers and temporal affections. For the sake of love, we put our hearts willingly in this crucible. We cry out, "Reveal what You must reveal in me, God. Do whatever You must do to cleanse my heart, silence my flesh, and draw me closer to You!"

Fasting Brings Humility

Fasting not only weakens us, it humbles us. King David said that he humbled himself with fasting (Ps. 35:13). Our bodies are tired, our minds are spacey, our strength is gone—our capacities are simply not at full operation. We find it difficult to do things we normally accomplish with ease. Yes, when we fast we are definitely not at our best in the natural realm. Most people find this humbling, not only in front of others, but within their own souls.

The heart of fasting is "afflicting our soul" (Is. 58:5). It might sound medieval, but it is a biblical way to express our desperate quest to encounter God more deeply. We do pay a certain price by giving up strength, comfort and pleasure. To top it off, fasting doesn't always seem to "work." Sometimes we fast without any immediately discernible results. This is even more humbling. We have to admit that we understand very little and we can control even less. However, part of humbling ourselves is to be determined to believe God's Word more than our natural senses, and to continue in prayer with fasting. We must be convinced that He is a rewarder of those who diligently seek Him (Heb. 11:6).

Overcoming Addictions to Legitimate Pleasures

There are three general categories of pleasures that stimulate our souls: illegitimate pleasures, pleasures that are legitimate, though not spiritually enhancing, and holy pleasures that come from living by the Word of God.

Unbelievers live primarily by *illegitimate sinful desires* and fantasy. They are driven by all kinds of imaginings of how much better their lives and futures will be if they keep acquiring better relationships, jobs, economic growth, etcetera.

It is obvious to believers that we must deny all of these illegitimate, sinful desires and fantasies (Matt. 16:24). Our greater challenge is in the area of *legitimate pleasures*. The norm in Christianity is to fill our lives with natural, permissible pleasures, such as honor, recreation, food, comfort and money, to prove that we are not religious. These are not sinful in themselves, but neither do they enhance our life in the Spirit. They do not bring us into greater contact with God.

At the highest level of life, the human spirit was created to live primarily by *the Word of God,* not by natural stimuli. Though our bodies need food, our souls are to be propped up and stimulated primarily by God's Word. "Man does not live by bread alone but by the Word of God" (Matt. 4:4).

We stimulate our souls in a multitude of ways rather than by God and by His Word. Our raw, naked weakness rarely gets exposed because we keep it propped up by things like food, entertainment, recreation, money, music, activity, and even ministry endeavors. Charles Finney, a powerful nineteenth-century evangelist, spoke about the deception of what he called "innocent amusements," declaring that too many people overindulge in entertainments that are not in and of themselves unrighteous, but that do not enhance their souls in fellowship with God.

Many believers are terrified at the thought of forsaking these stimulants to wait on God in the absolute rawness of their hearts. But how can we mourn for God when we have stuffed our souls with so much activity? In some cases our spirits are dulled to the point that we are barely aware of the fleshly movements of our hearts. Fasting involves deliberately silencing the pleasures of this world, even the legitimate ones, so that we may hear the voice of God's Word more clearly. Suddenly, we are conscious of our false drives, motives, and passions. As our egos are suppressed and our spirit tenderized through fasting, we will see our spirit man attain preeminence and live according to the realities and pleasures of the unseen world, instead of conforming to the spirit of the age.

Fasting Enhances Spiritual Pleasure

Fasting does not restrain our pleasure; it enhances it. Does this sound odd? We were raised in a culture that thinks backwards. We have been taught that we will experience more life if we pamper our bodies. This is wrong even on a purely natural level. Nutritionists tell us that the more we eat, the less sensitive our taste buds are. We actually taste less when we are not hungry. It's true. The more we indulge, the duller our senses grow. Moderation in the physical realm actually increases the pleasure we gain from physical activities. It makes sense that overindulging our bodies might detract not only from our physical enjoyment, but from our spiritual sensitivity as well. This puts our physical pleasures into proper perspective.

The truth is that our greatest pleasure comes by feasting on the Person of Jesus. Our pursuit of intimacy with Him involves fasting because it brings our body into its proper relationship with the life of the Spirit. Though our soul lives in a physical body, it was not designed to be a slave to physical pleasures and passions. If we want our spirit man to gain ascendancy over our flesh, we must deliberately silence the compulsions of our natural man. Only in properly denying some of the fleshly passions can both the physical and emotional aspects of our person experience the superior pleasures of life in the Spirit.

God ordained fasting to strengthen our physical life, not to frustrate it. We typically approach fasting as an activity that wages war against our bodies, when in fact it is intended to release them. It is *the world's system* that wages war against us, both physically and spiritually. God created our physical body to fast so that we may enter into the highest places in experiencing Him.

Fasting Regularly

Fasting is a gift that we should embrace more than occasionally. It is to be our lifestyle. It is not meant to be used as a shot in the arm several times a year, but was designed to be a consistent part of our lives, an available tool to expand our spiritual capacity for more of Jesus.

Fasting becomes easier the more we do it. The rhythm of our bodies actually changes when we fast regularly. It is similar to working out. When we don't exercise regularly and then start, it's difficult at first. Our cardiovascular system screams at us to slow down and our muscles are sore the next day. We have to exercise consistently for a season before our bodies adjust. In the same way, our bodies will acclimate and our emotions will change when we move into a natural rhythm of fasting.

The fear of fasting is worse than fasting itself. It is a lie that the demands of our modern pace of life make fasting impractical for today's Christian. In fact, fasting is neither too hard nor too uncomfortable for us. We may be tired, but the same grace God gave the believers of old will be given to us. In fact, at the end of the age there will be a much greater percentage of Christians entering into the grace of fasting than at any other time in history.

Entering the Wilderness

The fasted lifestyle is more than a concept or a new activity that we try out for awhile. It is a personal journey in our prayer life into the unfolding of greater and greater realms in God. This journey of prayer, strengthened and intensified by a life of fasting, can also be called "a wilderness lifestyle." Weakness and the wilderness are nearly synonymous. The wilderness in the Old Testament was a place of testing, training and meeting with God. In the wilderness, we leave everything behind to be sustained only by Him. There is nothing else out there but Him. In saying "yes" to a fasted lifestyle, we voluntarily enter the wilderness. We embrace natural weakness in order to gain supernatural strength.

God trained many of His choice servants in the wilderness. Moses was in the wilderness for about eighty years of his life. David matured in the wilderness. Joseph's prison experience was a wilderness time. Elijah retreated there, John the Baptist lived there, Paul spent three years there, and Jesus went there to fast.

One of the mysteries of God is that in our weakness in the wilderness we can find doorways into His strength. This mystery is revealed at the end of the Bride's journey in Song of Solomon. The Shulamite, a representation of the Bride, arises from the wilderness leaning on her Beloved Jesus. She has discovered the secret of His strength being made perfect in her weakness as she ascends from this journey of her life on Earth victoriously, leaning on His strength. "Who is this coming up from the wilderness, leaning upon her Beloved?" (Song 8:5).

In the wilderness of prayer and fasting, we face the barrenness of our own souls. This voluntary wilderness is the place of transformation. There we contend with God as Jacob did so that He will change us in the process. We voluntarily deny ourselves some of the "legitimate pleasures" in order to experience the "superior pleasures." The wilderness of fasting strips us of false comforts, strengths and securities. We come to grips with how much our souls are propped up by a thousand things other than God, and with how hard it is to feel love for Him or for others when those props are removed. Are we dulled under the spirit of the age without knowing it? Are we captive to the consumerism in our society? Are we blinded by too much eating, too much sleeping and too much entertainment? Are our hearts bloated and rigid from too little of the Word of God and too much of worldly comforts? The answer is most often yes. The solution is to enter the voluntary wilderness of prayer and fasting. As we are stripped of all other lovers, He transforms us into lovers of Him.

Kicking the Props Away

God ordained a time delay in our process of transitioning from inferior pleasures and sin to the superior pleasures of the gospel. We must transition into living primarily by the Word of God and secondarily by the legitimate pleasures God gives us, instead of the other way around, which is how most of us live now. We can have a life in God that is real, profound and powerful on the other end of the transition, a life in which we are primarily nourished, stimulated, and propped up by the Word of God. In this transition, there are obstacles to overcome. These hindrances *can be overcome* and this is the process of our transformation.

Once we've put on hold our normal, fleshly sources of comfort and support, we see our wretchedness and spiritual barrenness with true eyes. What was dormant rises to the surface. When all the props of comfort were taken away from those in the Superdome after Hurricane Katrina, we saw the rage that had been just one inch below the surface show its ugly face. This rage is in all of us without the grace of God. It is difficult to face these weaknesses, but after we touch more of God, even in small measures, we know that we can't go back to the old way of living stimulated predominately by the flesh.

Many of us experience a "dangling in-between" as we voluntarily fast from our old stimulants and comforts, but the spiritual stimulants have not yet come alive in us. For a season, we feel the raw emptiness of fasting but don't yet experience the superior pleasures in the Spirit. We have the vision of what is coming, in terms of a vibrant life in God, and the struggle of what is behind us, but we don't have the full reality yet. We have known a little foretaste of the realms we are to know in God, but that knowledge is not so dominant or prevailing that the struggle with our old addictions is · over. When we don't experience the superior pleasures that we're laboring for, we often go back to the old stimulants for comfort, only to discover they have lost their power because of our high vision in God. The old way does not have the strength to satisfy us and we do not yet have the capacity to receive the new way. We can feel ourselves dangling in between the two realms. Welcome to the fasted lifestyle!

We have not yet developed a capacity for the very thing we need for life and strength. We see this dynamic in the natural arenas of food, sunlight and exercise. Someone just rescued from starvation does not have the ability to digest most of the foods she may be immediately offered. A person who has been shut up in darkness for a long time craves sunlight, but its brightness is too painful to endure at first. One who has not exercised for years cannot work out heavily for many hours the first day without hurting himself. We are in a transition and our capacities must be enlarged to enter into that which we crave. This is all part of our journey forward in love. We have been brought here because of our desire for God. In the transformation process, He will answer our longing for Him ... but not right away.

In this transition, we are left for a time in the raw crankiness of free falling. In that place, God births humility. It is precious. Because of the difficulty of our own journey we are less disposed to have judgmental attitudes toward others. The whole process creates meekness in us as we continually remember the sweetness and the pain of our own journey. The transition period will end, though. According to Jesus, the poor in spirit and those who hunger and mourn after God, will be blessed and filled (Matt. 5:3-6).

The Lord wants to raise up a people who can speak with authority about finding joy in the wilderness. As the global Body of Christ enters this same transition at the end of the age, these forerunners will be able to articulate the vision of the knowledge of God and explain the details and reasons for the journey. They will be those who have walked the wilderness path first, and therefore can guide others with the wisdom learned from their own journeys with the Lord. People whose primary source is the Word of God give hope and courage to those who desire to enter into a deeper life in God. Their lives prove that it can be done. The fasted lifestyle is simply a life of regular prayer, fasting, giving, serving others, and blessing our enemies. The first step toward this life is to get a vision for having a deep life in God. John the Baptist was a forerunner who made his home in the wilderness. He lived in the spirit of prayer and fasting. God is pouring out that same spirit in this generation.

CHAPTER SIX

Five Expressions of the Fasted Lifestyle

Can you imagine what the people gathered around Jesus must have felt as He began to give His most important sermon, the sermon we now call the Sermon on the Mount? They were just people like you and me, with lives full of cares and concerns, questions and difficulties. I imagine all the types of men, women and children gathered around Jesus. On one side sits an older gentleman, somewhat sad in countenance, yet kind and tender-looking as well, a man who has lived many years under the cumbersome burdens of the Law. He has sought to bring his children up under these principles, and though one of his sons is indeed following in this way, two have rebelled in anger and contempt, and their hearts are estranged in bitterness from him even now. On the other side of Jesus I picture a young woman, a recent widow with pain still burning fresh in her heart. She hopes to find some ray of hope and light from whatever this new Teacher might say today.

The carpenter from Nazareth opens His mouth and begins to utter living truths and principles about the Kingdom of God that astonish His listeners. He speaks as one with authority, and as ordinary people hear His words, their hearts are stunned within them and their minds reel in perplexity. He teaches as none they have ever heard. The teachings of the scribes seemed as empty and forsaken tombs compared to the life and weight that exuded from every word of Jesus' mouth (Matt. 7:28-29). "Who is this Man?" they wonder. "What kind of authority is this?"

And what was it Jesus spoke that day that Matthew says was so astonishing? Did He utter lofty and indiscernible mysteries? Were His words so difficult and hard to comprehend that the men and women turned away confused and disheartened by their lack of understanding? No, the Sermon on the Mount, though filled with divine authority and eternal wisdom, could not be simpler in its presentation and application. Even the children gathered could understand. As they heard Jesus' words, and were amazed by His authority, I believe they were also astonished by the simplicity of what He introduced as the fundamental principles of the Kingdom.

The Sermon on the Mount Lifestyle

Many believers feel the Christian life is just too mysterious and difficult for them to really grasp, as if there were some well-kept secret of how to live abandoned for God that nobody ever told them. They look around and see godly men and women and think, "I truly must not get it. This only seems hard to me." There is a definite tension in the Kingdom of God, and we often run up against it in our pursuit of Him. The tension lies between the ease and the difficulty of a life of righteousness. Jesus said His yoke is easy and His burden light (Matt. 11:29-30), but He also said that the way is narrow and few find it: "Enter by the narrow gate; for wide is the gate and broad is the way that leads to destruction, and there are many who go in by it. Because narrow is the gate and difficult is the way which leads to life, and there are few who find it" (Matt. 7:13-14).

Are we to believe that the way of true Christianity is difficult on our flesh and that only a few find it? Yes, we are. While the true Christian life becomes easy on our spirit and is an easy burden once we decide to live by God's values, making the determination is not easy. It is difficult on our pride, lust and pocketbooks. It has an impact on day-to-day life, and it causes numerous relational conflicts for those who refuse to compromise—who refuse to go the broad way that leads to destruction (Matt. 7:13).

The difficult part of wholeheartedness is not in its mysteriousness. Jesus could not have made it more straightforward and simple. Wholeheartedness toward God, which we are meant to truly desire, is walked out by doing the main, plain things of Scripture. It is not complicated, but it is difficult to deny our fleshly desires and pride (Matt. 7:14). Jesus spelled out what wholeheartedness before God means in His Sermon on the Mount. Our way forward in love and bright righteousness is to live what I call a "Sermon on the Mount lifestyle" (Matt. 5-7).

What is this lifestyle? Jesus defined it as embracing godly attitudes (Matt. 5), as we give ourselves to prayer and the Word of God, with fasting, giving and serving others (Matt. 6). Serving others in love happens as we fellowship with believers and minister to unbelievers (Matt. 6-7). This calling of Jesus to all who respond in wholeheartedness is difficult in the actual tensions and frictions of walking out these principles in day-to-day life.

The Sermon on the Mount contains the non-negotiable principles, or "constitution," of the Kingdom of God. It defines the nature of true discipleship and is the standard by which spiritual maturity must be measured. A life or ministry not built on these principles will not stand under pressure (Matt. 7:24-27). The Sermon is meant to be taken literally. Its commands are simple and direct; it means what it says and it says what it means. At the same time, it is not to be understood or received apart from the central core motivations of our spiritual lives—love and desire.

These non-negotiable principles are set in place by the One who was crushed in death that we might have abundant life, all because of the raging love and passion in His heart. The Jesus who sat upon the mountain and delivered this message is the same Jesus who is our Bridegroom, burning with holy desire. The desire in His heart is imparted to our own hearts by the Holy Spirit, causing us to grow in love and live the Sermon on the Mount lifestyle. The secret of His burden being light is found in the love that fuels our hearts every day. Where love is present, the grueling quality of sacrifice and self-denial is absent.

Moses told the children of Israel to love God with all their heart (Deut. 30:6). He went on to explain that the path to loving Him wasn't mysterious (Deut. 30:11). No one has to be caught up into the third heaven to receive the blueprint for how to love God. Neither does anyone need to cross the seas to far away places to discover the secret steps to loving Him (Deut. 30:12-13). No, it is right here. It is written in our hearts and is as clear as the simple words spoken from our mouths (Deut. 30:14).

The pathway into abandonment to God is not complex, confusing or mysterious, but the very simplicity of Jesus' definition of wholehearted love can be a stumbling block. Some people wish it was an elusive life filled with secret principles, or a complicated commandment that only a few understood; then they would feel superior in their spiritual attainments. However, God designed His way for weak and broken people like us. Why? Because weak and broken people are the only kind of people who exist. We can all obey God's Word—and we can all be wholehearted in love. God's commandment is near us, in our hearts and in our mouths. And the Holy Spirit within, given as a gift at our new birth, is jealous to bring our hearts into this bright righteousness.

Five Expressions of the Fasted Lifestyle

So what does this Sermon on the Mount lifestyle look like in our day-to-day existence, and just how do we walk in voluntary weakness so that God's power may be perfected in our lives? There are five types of "fasting" described in the Sermon on the Mount. We fast _food, time, energy, money_ and _words_. Matthew 6:1-18 describes the five main activities of the fasted life that correspond with these. They include *giving, serving, praying* (with the Word), *blessing our enemies* and *fasting food.* Each is a form of fasting, in that we are voluntarily embracing weakness, declaring to God that we derive our life and strength from Him, and Him alone.

Jesus set forth these five activities as foundational to the Kingdom of God. By giving, we fast our money and financial strength. In serving and prayer, we are fasting our time and energy, investing it in others and in intercession. Blessing our enemies requires that we fast our words and reputation. In giving up food, we are fasting our physical and emotional strength.

Once again, unless done in a heart of love, these activities are empty and vain. They are also no substitute for pursuing 100-percent obedience. God does not keep score of our good works and bad works so that they may balance each other out. Some try to bargain with Him, promising to give more money or fast longer to make up for cheating on a financial deal or living in immorality. In the power of the Holy Spirit the prophet Samuel thundered against such dealing, declaring that the Lord loves obedience better than sacrifice (1 Sam. 15:22). True love for Jesus is demonstrated in our obedience to His will (John 14:15, 21-23). The Jesus who gave this call to the fasted lifestyle is the One who searches the motivations of our hearts. He is looking for love that is undivided and obedience that is pure. He has opened up His heart in this call and conveyed to us what He desires and requires from all of those who love Him. It is our marvelous privilege to respond.

The fasted lifestyle is a long-term commitment to these five expressions. No one graduates from these to go on to the "deeper things" of God. It is in the walking out of these five expressions, in the routine and mundane existence of our everyday lives, that we will reach the deepest places in intimacy with God. As we are consistently faithful to walking in these manifestations of the fasted lifestyle, we will chart our course down the narrow way of life, and we will discover the abundance of joy to be found there.

Giving

> When you do a charitable deed, do not let your left hand
> know what your right hand is doing, that your charitable
> deed may be in secret; and your Father who sees in secret
> will Himself reward you openly (Matt. 6:3-4).
>
> Do not lay up for yourselves treasures on earth, where moth
> and rust destroy and where thieves break in and steal; but
> lay up for yourselves treasures in heaven ... For where your
> treasure is, there your heart will be also ... No one can serve
> two masters; for either he will hate the one and love the other,
> or else he will be loyal to the one and despise the other. You
> cannot serve God and mammon (Matt. 6:19-24).

Jesus spoke about our charitable deeds, referring to both
financial giving and acts of servanthood. They are two of the five
expressions of fasting. Giving to others is fasting part of our money.
We are trusting God to return and multiply back to us the financial
strength that we have given away. We all know the story of the
widow who gave her last two mites. Jesus watched and admired,
and compared her to the wealthy, who only gave out of financial
surplus (Luke 21:1-4). They hardly missed the money they gave,
but the widow's gift cost her everything. It is important in the fasted
lifestyle to give in such a way that we feel its impact.

Money is a form of social and material strength. Our personal
resource base becomes weaker when we give it away. Instead of
using all our money on ourselves, we give all that we are able to
build God's Kingdom in others. We are investing in "God's bank,"
and this is an eternal investment with unmatched dividends. We
know God will return blessing to us in a great measure in this age
and in the age to come (Luke 6:38), though we don't always know
when or how. The exchange rate in this bank is highly favorable,
and we can give with confidence that God will reward us.

We actually get *more* use out of our money by giving it to help
build up Kingdom people and projects than we would ever get by

keeping it for ourselves. This giving may be hard temporarily, in that it is costly to give out of our lack rather than our surplus, but God has more than enough wealth to reward everyone 100-fold for their sacrifice. The benefits gained far outweigh the initial discomfort. Our obedience, trust and loyalty in the area of finances bring honor to the Lord. It is not just a quaint saying that God loves a cheerful giver (2 Cor. 9:6, 7). His heart moves when we sow bountifully and readily into the lives of others with certainty that He will replenish our lack. When we give joyously rather than grudgingly, because of our confidence in His generosity, we move the heart of the God whom we love.

Serving

Serving others is the second of the charitable deeds Jesus spoke about. In spending our time and energy on others we are fasting what we could have used to further our own interests. It is biblical to use a portion of our time and energy to provide for ourselves, our family, our business or ministry, or just our resource base in general. However, as we participate in charitable deeds—acts of kindness and service to others—we are spending that time for the benefit of others. This is at the heart of what it means to have a servant spirit. The time "wasted" in serving is time that we cannot use to jockey for position or establish our personal comfort and pleasure. Thus, we trust the Lord to work for our increase in a way that surpasses what we could have accomplished by spending that very same amount of time on establishing our name, cause and comfort. In the big picture, we get more done by investing time in serving and allowing God to reward our labors.

Jesus exemplified the life of servanthood more than anyone. He came not to be served but to serve (Matt. 20:28). He does not call us to anything that He Himself has not exceedingly surpassed us in doing. In the laying down of our lives for others, we are embracing what He embraced and thus embracing *Him.* Some of the sweetest intimacy with God can be found in pouring out our lives in service.

He did not call us to this simply because it is a good and godly way to live—but because in serving others we come face to face with the Servant of all.

Praying

"Pray to your Father who is in the secret place; and your Father who sees in secret will reward you openly" (Matt. 6:6). Jesus went on to call us to a life of prayer—the third expression of the fasted lifestyle. Prayer also is difficult in that our flesh so fights against the seeming lack of productivity. To pray to an invisible God is a taxing endeavor: the impact is usually delayed and is most often not discernible, and the reward promised by God is not always what we would have guessed.

Prayer and reading the Word of God are forms of voluntary weakness that fast our time and emotions (Matt. 6:5-13). Instead of using all of our time for the advancement of our status or success, we use some of it to seek the face of an invisible God. Instead of being entertained by the television or surfing the Internet, we intercede for those He loves.

When we give our time to God, we miss other opportunities to network; to build up our ministries, businesses, or personal status; or to recreate and be entertained. As I mentioned previously, in my early years I complained, "Lord, I could do a lot more for You if I did not have to spend time in prayer." It seemed like a waste. This type of fasting, though, is actually the opposite of "wasting" time. True, we have not used those hours to socialize, fellowship, or advance our position, but because of that, we are forced to entrust ourselves to the Lord for favor and promotion, and we quickly find that we will never be able to out-give God, even in issues of time and energy.

We are also fasting our emotional energy during prayer as we pour ourselves out and intercede for God's blessing on others. As we do this, we trust God to touch those we love. That would be reward enough. However, God also returns that very time and emotional energy to us in order to bless us personally. He often multiplies it via greater productivity. We get more done for others and ourselves by asking God than we would have accomplished by working without prayer. The time frame in which God rewards us with greater productively may not be not for years. You may sow ten or twenty years into prayer and suddenly God may open a door of opportunity for you to make more impact through prayer in one event or one season of life than during the prior twenty years. Some of that heightened productivity will not be seen until the age to come, but He does reward us during this age.

Pressing into a life of prayer and searching out His Word brings both difficulties and rewards. Though we fast our emotional energy and our time, we are brought into the fellowship of the burning heart of Jesus, the great Intercessor. We come alive on the inside by the encounters of love in the inner man that He pours out as we wait before Him. This call to prayer is arduous, but it also comes with the promise of a profound increase in our intimacy with God.

Blessing our Enemies

Love your enemies, bless those who curse you, do good to those who hate you, and pray for those who spitefully use you and persecute you (Matt. 5:44).

For if you forgive men their trespasses, your heavenly Father will also forgive you (Matt. 6:14).

Another part of the fasted lifestyle is seen in blessing and forgiving our enemies. This is an expression of fasting related to our relationships and position before people. When we bless our enemies, we are fasting our words and reputation. This might be a new idea to some. To avoid speaking negative words about our enemies is a true fast. Our silence can hurt our reputation because we refuse to come to our own defense. A good reputation is part of the strength of our life and we all have a strong drive for self-preservation and self-promotion.

Instead of making full use of our words to defend and promote ourselves, the Lord calls us to restrain our speech and focus on others, including blessing our enemies. An "enemy" in the most general sense is one who blocks our goals. They speak and act in ways that hinder our plans and purposes. What our enemies do often results in us losing honor, time, money and even relationships. No one appreciates this loss.

However, the Lord calls us to act in the opposite spirit when we encounter such a loss. Just as He did, we must actively forgive and bless our enemies. This means refraining from words that would have exposed our enemy, defended our position, and strengthened us with the sympathy and support of others. When we lose that natural strength, imitating the Lord's silence before His accusers, we are forced to gain our strength and comfort from God. Blessing others in the face of their accusation requires that we entrust ourselves to God. This is rare. To be silent and let God answer on our behalf is perhaps the most difficult form of fasting.

Our selfishness has to die before we are able to leave our defense completely in God's hands. Refusing to speak against those who mistreat us goes against our natural tendency of self-preservation. Jesus committed Himself to God to make things right when men reviled and threatened Him. In this Jesus trusted God to vindicate Him in the right way and at the right time. "When He was reviled, did not revile in return; when He suffered, He did not threaten, but committed Himself to Him who judges righteously" (1 Pet. 2:23).

When we bless our enemies, we give up the right to the emotional and social strength we might have gotten from fighting back. We fast from defending our reputation, and trust the Lord to fight for us when we are silent. This is perhaps the expression of the fasted lifestyle taken the least literally by believers. We think, surely God would not want me to be silent right now when that person is so overtly wrong! He would want the truth to win out, right? Confident that we are doing the right thing, we speak to defend ourselves and expose our enemies. Yet God's invitation is to willingly and completely entrust Him with our reputations and our relationships.

Fasting from Food

"When you fast, anoint your head ... so that you do not appear to men to be fasting, but to your Father who is in the secret place; and your Father who sees in secret will reward you openly" (Matt. 6:17-18). Finally, Jesus calls us to the fasting of food. Abstaining from food is what we typically think of when we refer to fasting. As mentioned earlier, the great difficulty of fasting food is not so much hunger as it is weakness—our natural strength is diminished when we fast from food. When our flesh rises up against fasting, it is not only because we are hungry and want to go gorge ourselves; it is because we are tired of feeling physically and mentally weak. We do not like feeling this way. It is a burden. Giving our physical strength to God is not only a burden; it can cause us to miss opportunities.

The paradox of fasting becomes apparent again as we realize and believe that in the grace of God we will get more done by investing our energy in fasting food than we would have accomplished by working without fasting. The energy "used up" in fasting is not used to comfort our bodies. We are forced to entrust ourselves to the Lord for both strength and comfort, and as we do so, we become focused on encountering God. And though there is most often a delay element in seeing the rewards of fasting, the wisdom of surrendering ourselves to the Lord in this way is no less real.

Five Different Types of Food Fasts

There are five common categories of fasting food. First, a *regular fast* is one in which we go without food, drinking only water or liquids that have no calories. Common lengths for this fast are one day, three days, or one week. It occasionally is longer, sometimes twenty-one days or even forty days.

Second, a *liquid fast* is one in which we go without solid foods and drink only light liquids, such as fruit juices. Most people do not include milk shakes in this type of fast.

Third, an *absolute fast*, sometimes called an Esther fast, is one in which we abstain from all food and water. This fast lasts for one to three days. I encourage people to be cautious when going on an absolute fast and to never extend it beyond three days.

The fourth type of fast, a *partial fast,* sometimes called a Daniel fast, is one in which we abstain from tasty foods and eat only certain things, like vegetables or nuts. John Wesley often fasted on bread and water. Those with hypoglycemia or other medical conditions can engage in a partial fast by being creative. We also encourage people to embrace a media fast in which they abstain from media entertainment, excluding news.

Fifth, a *Benedict Fast,* established by Saint Benedict of Nursia, Italy (525 AD), is one in which we eat only one meal a day. Many monks in the monasteries of Europe lived this way for years and had strong bodies and even stronger spirits.

The Fasted Lifestyle is Normal Christianity

Possibly the greatest enemy of and lie about the fasted lifestyle in the Body of Christ is the false notion that fasting is *radical Christianity,* an optional exercise for the healthy Christian life. It is not. Fasting is normal and basic to the Christian life—it is Christianity 101. Yet most of us grew up in settings where fasting was rarely mentioned. It was either ignored or treated as something unusual; but there is no such thing as New Testament Christianity without regular fasting.

It is not possible to live biblical Christianity without being committed to a lifestyle of praying, fasting, giving, serving, and blessing our enemies. A form of Christianity devoid of any of these five elements is not New Testament Christianity. We are all called to fast regularly. There are obvious exceptions; people who are pregnant or have health problems should consult their doctors before fasting from food. But the rule of the Christian life is to fast regularly, and even if someone cannot fast from food because of health issues, there are still four other ways in which they can fast. There is no Bible passage that excludes 21st century people in the

Western world from the Sermon on the Mount lifestyle because we are too busy or too important, or for any other reason. When we come face to face with Jesus one day, He will not make an exception for us because we lived in the 21st century. What He called the early Church to do is what He calls all believers to do, and He provides the same grace to us to respond.

Some of us have a distorted idea of grace. We think that if our activities are motivated by grace they will be easy. Jesus said that His yoke is easy (Matt. 11:29-30). It is easy because in our weakness we can have confidence that we are acceptable and pleasing to God. It is easy because we do not have to produce anything to receive God's enjoyment. God helps to motivate and sustain us and gives us confidence that He delights in our obedience and will reward us in eternity for it. It is easy to be in God's favor and receive His love. Thus, on one hand, Christianity is easy.

Yet, on the other hand, the way is difficult. Jesus said to enter by the narrow gate, a gate that is difficult but leads to life. Only a few find it (Matt. 7:13-14). It takes a resolute heart to stay the course over the months and years. Grace does not mean that the way will never be hard. It means God will always supply what we need to walk in it.

I am deeply committed to calling people to live this Sermon on the Mount lifestyle, and to respond to it as Christianity 101. I encourage our staff members at IHOP-KC to pursue the Lord in prayer, using the Word. I urge them to read ten chapters of the New Testament each day. In doing this, they will read through the entire New Testament once each month. I urge them to fast at least one day a week. Two days a week is better. In the financial arena, I encourage them to give beyond their tithes and more than out of their surplus, and to give until they feel the cost of giving. I also exhort them to serve others and bless their enemies. These are all part of normal Christianity and should not be treated as optional or unimportant. Our treasure in heaven does not correspond just to our giving habits here on Earth, but is laid up as we engage in all five of these Kingdom activities day in and day out (Matt. 6:19-20). God esteems and remembers these acts for eternity.

CHAPTER SEVEN

Fasting to Break Spiritual Strongholds

The False God of Food

One of the most significant things Jesus said concerning the power of fasting is recorded in the Book of Matthew. His disciples could not cure a demonized boy and the boy's father came to Jesus for deliverance. The disciples were perplexed as to why they could not cast the demon out and Jesus told them that a lifestyle of prayer and fasting was the key: "'Lord, have mercy on my son, for ho is an epileptic and suffers severely; for he often falls into the fire and often into the water. So I brought him to Your disciples, but they could not cure him.' ... Jesus rebuked the demon, and it came out of him; and the child was cured from that very hour. Then the disciples came to Jesus privately and said, 'Why could we not cast him out?' Jesus said ... , 'This kind does not go out except by prayer and fasting'" (Matt. 17:15-21). In essence, Jesus was telling the disciples that the anointing to break Satan's power over the lives of His people was linked to prayer and fasting. Fasting is one of the necessary elements we should embrace when we confront demonic strongholds.

There is a false god that must be dethroned in our lives—the god of physical appetites, specifically the god of *food.* This god undermines the cross of Christ. Philippians 3:18-19 says, "For many ... are enemies of the cross of Christ: whose end is destruction and whose god is their belly... " Food, which is a God-ordained blessing, has been exploited by demonic powers. Paul addressed this false god, which had established a spiritual stronghold in some people in the New Testament Church. He said their god was their belly, their physical appetites.

As shocking as it seems, we have given real territory in our lives over to demons by allowing food to be an idol in our lives. Paul put his finger right on this idol and called it a false god. It usually goes unrecognized today. Believers in the Western Church allow this god to reign in their lives uncontested, day in and day out, and do not realize that through indulgence they are worshipping something other than the one, true God.

No one thinks they worship food; no Christian wants to worship food. Yet our appetites—our desire to eat—can preoccupy our schedules and plans to the point where it becomes one of our primary life goals. Some think about food continually, imagining what they will eat next and ordering their days around it. They don't even recognize they have been caught in the snare of putting their trust in food. This false trust manifests itself when we eat to calm our nerves; to have the courage to face our fears; to cover the reality of our internal struggles; and to feel comfort and joy. If you were honest, what would you say is the primary source people use to calm their nerves, relieve their fears, distract them from their problems, and bring them joy? Without question it is a *god*, an idol and a spiritual stronghold.

It is easy to see the truth of this stronghold in people who obsess over food—those who talk about it most of the time and those who are continually thinking about it. We think we are not caught in this trap, but the snare is found in the subtle nature of this deception. Though we are not bowing down, singing praise songs, and worshipping our bellies, we may be more ensnared than we think. We may be way more emotionally attached and mentally connected to food than we would like to admit, and without question, we need the grace of fasting to both dethrone this idol and to protect us from it taking root in our lives.

How much of a stronghold it has in our lives won't become apparent until we begin to fast regularly. If you are not sure if an overindulgent love for food is really a spiritual stronghold in your life, watch what happens when food is taken away. Rage immediately surfaces. The children of Israel rebelled because they were tired of eating only manna day after day in the wilderness. They became willing to cast off their covenant with God and go back to Egyptian slavery just to have tasty food again. The measure of our discomfort and anger when we are denied food's pleasure and comfort is the measure of our worship and adoration of it.

The paradoxical reality of food is that God created it with all the complications of its proper use and abuse. He knew the complex nature of this gift, yet gave it to us to handle. Why would the Lord allow something so prominent to have such a perilous cutting edge to it? It is a paradox that causes us to tremble. The Lord wants voluntary lovers, those who will disavow their supreme loyalty to food, comfort and ease that they might enter into the fullness of God.

Food is good, not innately evil. Our physical appetites are God-given; food is one of His great gifts to us. He created it to provide strength and to be a means of celebrating His goodness, both during this age and the age to come (Luke 22:16-18). In order to participate in these two godly purposes of food—physical strength and the celebration of God's goodness—we need *discernment*. We need to proceed *carefully* because that which is good in its proper balance becomes the *object of idolatry* when we participate in it in an unrighteous manner. This blessing of food and drink has great potential to lead us away from its natural purpose when demonic powers exploit it. On one hand, we celebrate receiving strength, pleasure and fellowship through it. On the other hand, overindulgence in it will allow the enemy to gain territory in our lives that leads to demonic strongholds and tremendous destruction.

To understand how food can sabotage our life in God, we must first consider how God has created us. Our bodies play a significant role in our spiritual lives. They were designed by God to be vehicles through which we experience Him. Because of this, our bodies, souls and spirits are deeply interrelated. It is by God's design that our emotional life, our spiritual capacities, and our physical appetites dynamically overlap, interact with and affect one another. We cannot separate our spirit from that which we feed our emotional and mental lives, or from what we do with our physical appetites. Our souls prosper when our bodies are under the control of the Holy Spirit, but our spirit becomes dull and grieved when they are not.

Our body is the temple of the Holy Spirit. If it is dominated by sin, our ability to experience God's life is quenched. We defile both our spirit and body if we yield to our physical appetites in an ungodly way. Some things in this category are obvious, such as alcohol, drugs, and sexual immorality. However, this potential defilement also occurs when lawful appetites are brought to excess in our lives. The definition of excess is different for each person, and may change with different seasons in our lives. Most of us easily see the connection between sinful actions and the defilement of our spirit, but often do not connect overindulgence of legitimate appetites to our spiritual dullness. We must realize they are deeply and profoundly connected.

Many believers in the Western world are caught in the snare of being preoccupied with eating, entertainment and recreation. It is not uncommon for countless men and women who consider themselves godly people to pursue a life of ease in the same way the world does, all the while believing that the grace of God entitles them to such things. Our spirits are crying to enter into divine ascent, to soar with the Holy Spirit as we were created to, but we have stuffed our souls and our bodies in a way that shuts down our spirit and entrenches us in defilement of the flesh.

Fasting food is a brilliant strategy of God. Though at first we wonder why we should fast from that which God gave us for strength and celebration, we find that the way we enter into more of God's blessing is by receiving these blessings in their right measure, not allowing them to become strongholds of idolatry in our lives. Fasting serves this purpose by keeping the blessing of food in check and freeing our spirits to reach the heights of intimacy with God.

Spiritual Bondage Through Food

This false god of food has operated throughout human history, affecting pagans and the people of God alike. The first hint of it was when Satan tempted Eve in the Garden of Eden. The enemy presented her with something that touched her physical appetite and the delightfulness of the fruit added to Eve's temptation to cross a God-given boundary of the knowledge of good and evil (Gen. 3:6). We see this stronghold again when the Lord addressed the idol of food in Ezekiel's generation, saying that Israel had fallen to the sin of Sodom partly by having been overcome with an excessive indulgence in food, along with other excesses. "This was the iniquity of your sister Sodom: She ... had pride, fullness of food, and abundance of idleness; neither did she strengthen the hand of the poor" (Ezek. 16:49).

We generally think of the sin of Sodom as immorality, but immorality was the byproduct of the other underlying sins. The sin of Sodom consisted of four things: their fullness of food, abundance of idleness and covetousness that refused to help the poor, all stemming from a pride that misused food, time and money. These were the tentacles that reached down into the human spirit to pull up a cesspool of sexual perversion.

This stronghold of food was also alive and well in the generation of Israel that God brought out of Egypt. God faithfully fed them with manna that fell from heaven, but they wanted a change of diet. "Now the mixed multitude who were among them yielded to intense craving; so the children of Israel also wept again and said: 'Who will give us meat to eat? We remember the fish which we ate freely in Egypt, the cucumbers, the melons, the leeks, the onions, and the garlic; but now our whole being is dried up; there is nothing at all except this manna before our eyes!'" (Num. 11:4-6).

The Lord brought the people out of the land and the people yielded to the intense cravings of physical appetites. Though they had manna from God, they cried out for a change of diet, wanting meat, garlic, leaks, and other tasty foods. Their problem was not that they were hungry, but that they wanted the taste and pleasure of food. They said their *beings were dried up* because they did not have tasty food. They wept bitterly before God, saying they were willing to go back to Egyptian slavery for the sake of these savory things.

These are the same people who witnessed the ten plagues of Egypt and the parting of the Red Sea. A pillar of fire led them by night and a cloud by day. Yet they were willing to reject the Divine promises, their calling and God's miracles on their behalf, all for tasty food. They were willing to dismiss seeing the glory of God's fire, the cloud of smoke, and even the prophetic promises that their children would enter into—all for *taste*. How real is the god of food? The Israelite's beings had not really dried up in the way they complained, but they did dry up spiritually after God gave them what they wanted. He sent leanness into their souls (Ps. 106:15).

The children of Israel voiced what we in the Western Church would never be able to acknowledge openly, and perhaps what we don't even realize: the god of food has enslaved our hearts and established a stronghold. Slavery is perilous. It means that we are possessed by a master or masters other than the Lord. It is so easy to distance ourselves from these stories and think ourselves more spiritual or more mature in God, yet we are as greedy today for our physical pleasures as the Israelites were then.

The culture of immorality in Sodom, and in Israel during Ezekiel's day, is the same as that of the Western world today, and the craving the Israelites had for the tasty foods of Egypt can be found in almost every house, grocery store and food advertisement in our nation. This spirit permeates our culture. These physical appetites are not neutral, innocent or harmless when they are outside the will of God; rather they are damaging and powerful, and the Western Church knows little about it. Though God does not love us less because of our participation in this, our spirits are dulled by it. When we surrender our passion to the idols of food and ease, we submit ourselves to their power over our lives, and become slaves to their dominion. This idolatry has not been confronted in the western Church in a significant way. The reality is that this is a spiritual war that has escaped our notice.

Jesus addressed this perilous reality in the parable of the foolish, rich farmer (Luke 12:16-20). The farmer wanted to live a life of ease, enjoying food and wine, with little concern for the will of God. He certainly did not want to enter into the burden of the purposes of God. In the parable, the Lord called him a fool. He lived for his money, food and free time so he could indulge himself in comfort and pleasure.

Many today have the same goal. They want to escape the pressures of life through merriment. Even some in the Church are willing to give up their spiritual future for the pleasures of food and ease now. Those in the Western Church will gather to worship and hear the Word on Sunday, as long as the service does not go longer than an hour, so they can go eat and play. In fact, we will gather to do almost anything besides pray and fast. The stronghold of food is strangling our hearts and we must respond to the Lord's invitation to become free of it. My point is not to scold, but to shake us awake to the reality that we are probably not as dedicated to God as we imagine ourselves to be.

The condition of the Church today demands that we dethrone the god of food and begin to embrace lifestyles of prayer with fasting. The Church has become content with being unable to heal the sick or free the people we pray for from demons. It has become normal for sin to destroy families and marriages. The prayer rooms are empty, powerful evangelism is rare, and unbelievers do not tremble before the Church as they did in the Book of Acts. Our preaching is often powerless and people pleasing. Yet, for all of this, there are few who clearly see what is going on. Let us not have shriveled souls any longer. Instead of continuing in lives trapped in bondage to pleasure, entertainment, and recreation, we must begin to pray and fast with consistency. God promises that if we will enter into fasting and prayer, He will deliver us from our bondage and bring us into lives freed from the lusts of the age and the strongholds of food, comfort and ease.

Tearing Down the Stronghold of Physical Appetites

Food is a very disappointing pleasure in one sense, because its satisfaction is so superficial and temporal, but it can be spiritually powerful and seductive. We have to confront its power in our lives. Clearly, the path out of this captivity includes fasting and prayer. But most are nearly paralyzed by the fear of fasting. I remember this initial fear in my personal journey when I first said "yes" to God's call to live a fasted lifestyle. I was petrified. I soon found, however, that the fear of fasting is worse than fasting itself.

Jesus fasted for forty days when He went into the wilderness to be tested (Matt. 4). The fast was not part of His testing, but part of the process that strengthened Him to stand against Satan's temptations. The early Church commonly engaged in fasting in order to withstand the enemy. Many of the saints throughout history have understood that God's Spirit-ordained fasting is a powerful way to counter the unique attack of Satan that comes during seasons of God's special anointing. Fasting combined with agreement with God, which is repentance, and focused meditation on the Word result in our mind's strongholds being pulled down. "For the weapons of our warfare are not carnal but mighty in God for pulling down strongholds" (2 Cor. 10:4).

The false god of food resists fasting and prayer. Demonic powers know that fasting is a powerful tool in spiritual warfare, so it is in their best interest to keep us in bondage to food and thus unable to wield this explosive weapon. John the Baptist was attacked for his lifestyle of radical fasting. Jesus said that John came neither eating nor drinking and they thought he was demonized (Matt. 11:18). John was perceived as dangerous and deluded because of his message and his lifestyle of fasting and prayer. The same spirit that attacked John the Baptist empowers the whole of our immoral Western culture. It will not go away quietly. It came against John, and it will attack those who dedicate themselves to prayer and fasting in this generation. It will ultimately be unsuccessful against those who consistently live the fasted lifestyle.

Warring Against Besetting Sins through Prayer and Fasting

"Let us lay aside every weight, and the sin which doth so easily beset us, and let us run with patience the race that is set before us" (Heb. 12:1, KJV). Fasting is not only an aid in deliverance from addictions to our physical appetites. God has also given this grace to us for the pulling down of demonic strongholds in our minds. God wants to free us from "besetting sins" and the lies about our identity that entrap us.

Besetting sins are more serious than sins into which we stumble on occasion. They are habitual actions or attitudes that hold God's people in bondage. Paul spoke of this as being captured by the snare of the devil (2 Tim. 2:26). Common sins that beset people include pornography, immorality, anger, alcohol, drugs, tobacco and different eating disorders, such as either eating too much or too little. Isaiah exhorts us to fast to "loose the bonds of wickedness" (Is. 58:6), that we might be freed from the sinful behavior to which we are addicted. Those struggling with a besetting sin feel helpless before their particular addiction. Some fall into great depression and despair, and are unable to see a way of escape. Willpower is not strong enough to break us free of besetting sins. Strongholds are demonically energized; they are established on territory Satan has been given rights to hold, either through our sin or the sin of those in the generations before us.

Christians feel hopeless when they spend years attempting to be good and strong, but still cannot overcome their eating disorder, or get free from Internet pornography, or stop drinking, or break out of an immoral relationship. They cry out to God, go to counseling and jump in every prayer line, but freedom does not come. How then can we be freed from such strongholds in our lives? We must acknowledge the source of spiritual strongholds if we want to break their hold over us, and use the spiritual weapons the Lord has given instead of our own carnal ones. We must sincerely repent of our involvement with each specific area of darkness in our lives.

We open the door to spiritual strongholds through our sin, ungodly values or occult activity, and stay connected to them especially by bitterness or wrong ideas and thinking. Bitterness is a sin that keeps us bound to those who mistreated us (Matt. 18:21-35). Ungodly values, mindsets and sins can exert spiritual control over a family line for generations. Other people fall under the power of spiritual strongholds through involvement with the occult, séances, spiritism, astrology, or black or white magic. We must include in this list our own contribution to self-deception. We have chosen to stay entrenched in darkness by neglecting to fill ourselves with the truths of God's Word.

Regardless of how we are involved, we must ruthlessly repent of all that we've done to allow spiritual strongholds and to give the enemy rights to territory in our lives. If we ask in faith, the Holy Spirit will reveal to us what strongholds Satan has and what areas of darkness we perpetuate through the sin of our wrong mindsets. Our ability to repent, to resist the devil, and to walk in the truth of the Word and in the power of the Holy Spirit, is deepened as we fast and pray.

We must not neglect fasting and prayer as parts of this journey to overcome addictive sins and demolish strongholds. Many of the counseling ministries in the Church today look down on prayer and fasting as being unnecessary, offering instead what they believe to be more "practical" means of deliverance. However, Jesus stressed the place of prayer with fasting in the struggle against sin and bondage (Matt. 17:21). Are our counselors wiser and more sophisticated than Jesus? I would not send anyone to a counseling ministry that did not value prayer and fasting. Though ministries that do value prayer and fasting are hard to find in the Church today, God is raising up more all the time.

Warring Against Besetting Sins Through the Word

Our effectiveness in prayer and fasting is dynamically connected to our depth in the Word of God. Paul said the Word effectively works in us to deliver us from besetting sins (1 Thess. 2:13). Why is it so effective? Because the Word of God is living and powerful, and sharper than any two-edged sword as it breaks bondages in our lives (Heb. 4:12). Prayer and fasting make us more open to the Word living in us and working in us. John 15:7 says, "If My words abide in you, you will ask what you desire, and it shall be done for you." James 1:21 says, "Lay aside all filthiness and receive with meekness the implanted word, which is able to save (deliver) your souls." Jesus promised that if God's words, which are His thoughts, abide in us, we would have power in prayer. The Word abides in us as we meditate on Scripture and pursue 100-percent obedience. The Word abides in us when it takes root in our mind. The fuel for the spirit of prayer is the Word of God saturating our inner man.

We do not want to just "say our prayers" in a religious, mechanical way. Some fast as if it were a sort of magical trick to remove sin from the heart. They do not repent or fill themselves with God's Word. Fasting in itself does not change us; the power of God does. Storing up God's Word in our hearts is the way to freedom from earthly or sinful delights and the way to freedom and delight in God. As this happens, we will be able to lay our false gold in the dust, rejoice in God alone, and see our prayers accomplished.

Lay up His Words in your heart. If you return to the Almighty ... then you will lay your gold in the dust ... Yes, the Almighty will be your gold ... for then you will have your delight in the Almighty ... You will make your prayer to Him, He will hear you ... You will declare a thing, and it will be established for you ... (Job 22:22-28).

Establishing an Action Plan to be in the Word

Each of the 400 staff members at the International House of Prayer Missions Base in Kansas City sit in the Prayer Room a certain number of hours per week. I have suggested some simple guidelines to help them to stay focused during the times they are not actively engaging with the worship team or praying on the microphone. We can use these guidelines outside the prayer room as well. We must believe that it is God's will for us to have a dynamic prayer life. Let me suggest a simple but effective action plan for spiritual development.

First, establish a personal Bible study plan to fill your heart with the Word until it becomes alive in you. If you find the Word boring, then press through. Do not give up until you feel its power in your heart. Reading ten chapters of the New Testament six days a week is a simple way to read through the entire New Testament each month. I also encourage the staff to take Bible school classes. We offer them through the Internet, as do many other Bible schools. Attend Bible studies at your church, school or workplace. Some people study more when they go to Bible teachings with others. Read biographies of people who lived dedicated lives and operated in the power of the Holy Spirit. Study the individual books of the Bible using at least two commentaries to help you understand them. Read Christian books that give you practical insight and encourage you in godliness.

Second, pray much in the Spirit. I encourage all to try to pray in the Spirit for one hour a day, while focusing on the Throne of God as described in Revelation 4. It is important to journal while doing this. Paul said that when we pray in the Spirit, we edify our spirit and receive mysteries (revelation) from God (1 Cor. 14:2, 4). Praying in the spirit was so important to Paul that he prayed this way more than anyone else (1 Cor. 14:18). Paul wrote, "For he who speaks in a tongue does not speak to men but to God ... however, in the spirit he speaks mysteries ... He who speaks in a tongue edifies himself ... " (1 Cor. 14:2-4); and "I thank my God I speak with tongues more than you all" (1 Cor. 14:18).

Third, schedule regular fasting days. I urge all to fast at least once a week. It is better to fast two days a week. Also, go on a long fast occasionally.

Fourth, develop a personal prayer list. This will help you focus as you pray through it each day. Praying out loud helps me to control my thoughts. Even praying at a whisper makes a difference. My personal prayer list has three main areas. First, I pray for a *breakthrough for my heart.* I focus on growing in intimacy by asking the Lord to release in me the anointing to love. This includes the Spirit helping me to understand and feel God's love and then to love Him in return (Eph. 3:16-19). I ask for the fear of God to be released to me (Ps. 86:11), and that I might learn meekness from Jesus (Matt. 11:29). We must imitate what Job did when he made a covenant with his eyes to walk in purity (Job 31:1; Ps. 101:3). Part of the breakthrough in the heart involves asking for divine help to control our speech (Ps. 141:3; James 3:2). In all this I want to hear God clearly and obey Him promptly.

Second, I pray for a *breakthrough for my mind.* I ask God for wisdom and direction for each of the specific areas of my life and ministry, then for the revelation of the Word of God (Eph. 1:17-18). Specifically, I ask to understand God's personality and purposes. I want to know His emotions (Ps. 27:4) and will for my life and ministry (Col. 1:9). I ask for revelation of God's end-time purposes (Dan. 11:35; 12:10).

Third, I ask God for a *breakthrough of power on my ministry.* I ask for anointed hands and words. I want God's power to flow through us all in healings and miracles. I also ask for apostolic power on my words, that the conviction of the Spirit will rest on them whether I am praying, preaching or in personal conversations with friends or unbelievers. I ask for prophetic insight to perceive the secrets of men's hearts so I might minister effectively to them (1 Cor. 14:25). I use the New Testament prayers of the apostles for each of these areas. There are many different prayer lists on IHOP-KC's Web site to help you get started.

Fifth, develop a prayer list that focuses on praying for others. Pray specifically for God's breakthrough in various areas of their lives. Include on this list family, friends, ministries, the unsaved, the sick, etc. Pray through the same three areas outlined above in my personal prayer list.

One word of exhortation is to use your evenings to strengthen your spirit. Many believers diminish their life in God in the evenings, then seek to recover spiritual ground during the day. Evening is the time when most spiritual loss takes place and spiritual ground is given up. We must not continually take one step forward and one step back. The territory that we gain in spiritual warfare can be lost again through neglect or sin. Let us be diligent in prayer, fasting, and abiding in the Word. Only then will we see the enemy's strongholds progressively demolished in our lives and the power and love of God begin to be more and more manifest in our experience.

CHAPTER EIGHT

Five Rewards of the Fasted Lifestyle

(Dana speaking) When I really felt the Lord's invitation to say "yes" to the grace of fasting several years ago, I remember trembling at even the thought of it. It seemed like a mountain in front of me. I found it difficult to connect with why this was so important in the Christian life and even more difficult to imagine that there might actually be rewards experienced by doing it. However, the Lord soon surprised me, as He loves to do when we say "yes" to this invitation.

As I began to incorporate regular fasting into my schedule, I realized, little by little, that fasting was not the drudgery I had imagined. Not only that, but there were parts of it that were wonderful. For example, I loved the tenderness I felt before God in times of fasting, the sensitivity and love for the Lord that rested on my heart. Progressively, God began to win me over by allowing me to experience the benefits of fasting. I grew to value and love it to such a degree that I now crave it. This is perhaps one of the most surprising realities I have encountered in fasting: receiving the grace to actually love it.

Fasting by nature has no drawing power. As those who were

created for pleasure, by a God of pleasures unending, we are not naturally drawn to this sort of discipline. Before I encountered some of the very real benefits to be found in fasting, I would have never imagined that it could be even remotely possible to love fasting. But it is possible, and probable, when these rewards begin to touch our hearts. Though I know I have barely scratched the surface of the depths of these wonderful benefits, I believe with all my heart in their very real existence. My desire is to spend the rest of my days, by the grace of God, responding to the invitation of fasting and receiving the rewards of fasting. Jesus beckons each one of us to partake of this invitation (Matt. 6:17, 18).

Fasting Brings Internal Rewards

"When you fast ... do not appear to men to be fasting ... your Father who sees in secret will reward you openly" (Matt. 6:17-18). Saying "yes" to the fasted lifestyle and positioning our hearts before a Bridegroom God in fasting is a marvelous invitation from the Lord, and there are many rewards to be reaped from doing so. What we must know from the beginning of this journey, however, is that many of these rewards are at first hidden from us because they are internal rewards, related to our intimacy with God. They are centered around that which touches the heart and thus are often difficult to recognize easily or quickly. Transformation is occurring in us that we cannot immediately detect, but it is nonetheless real. These benefits often carry a "delay element" in that we cannot recognize them until we look back in retrospect. Knowing about this delay factor in advance allows us to resist discouragement at what appears to be a lack of breakthrough when we first start fasting.

To many people, it might be a new concept to pursue God for rewards that are primarily internal. Some people only approach fasting as a way to increase God's power in their ministry. It is biblical to fast for this purpose (Matt. 17:21). However, the one who fasted more than anyone else in Scripture, besides Anna, was John the Baptist, who did no miracles, signs or wonders (John 10:41).

Yet Heaven's view of John was amazing. Gabriel prophesied that he would be great in the sight of God, and Jesus called him the greatest man ever born of a woman (Luke 1:15; Matt. 11:11). His greatness was not related to miracles in his ministry. He did not do any. His greatness was found in his obedience to and intimacy with God, which He cultivated by living a fasted lifestyle.

Without an understanding of the transformation God will bring to us through fasting, we might be prone to fear it. Many are only aware of the negative and difficult side of fasting. The new information to most is that fasting brings amazing benefits with regard to our intimacy with God. In this chapter, we will focus on five rewards in fasting—benefits so powerful that they will eventually cause us to love fasting! Have we ever imagined fasting could be exhilarating? It is *only* because we have a beautiful God and a Bridegroom who burns with desire toward us. The surprise awaiting us is the exhilaration of feeling His joy and desire toward us. We will eventually become so hungry to increase our experience of God's presence that we will fast even more. Fasting is not an experience to fear, but one into which we should eagerly jump. Before the Lord returns, it will be common for those who love Him to also love fasting.

Reward #1: Fasting tenderizes and sensitizes our hearts to receive more of God.

Fasting tenderizes our emotions. By nature, our hearts are prone to hardness and dullness toward the Lord. Because we are either moving toward God or away from Him, with there being no neutral ground, we can subtly develop spiritual dullness without even realizing it. We often unconsciously begin to slowly move from spiritual tenderness to dullness. When we come to grips with this alarming propensity in our heart, then we begin to take the call to fasting seriously. Fasting before a Bridegroom sensitizes and softens our hearts.

This tenderizing of the heart is something that is hard to

recognize at first. It's not initially blatant or intense, so we can't always perceive its progress. Sometimes only when we look back in retrospect can we perceive how soft He has made our hearts before Him through the grace of fasting.

Over time we find an increased anointing to bring the first commandment into first place in our lives: we begin to love God with all our hearts, souls, minds and strength. We increase in our ability to feel and experience God's affection and beauty. We feel His love for us and we feel love for Him in return. What experience in life could be more powerful than this? Not only are we catching a greater glimpse of His beauty, we're also seeing our own beauty in Him. This back-and-forth interaction is the foundation of divine romance. We encounter and experience the superior pleasures of the gospel. Nothing thrills and frees the human heart more than the exhilarating feeling that comes when the Spirit communicates the love of Jesus to our hearts.

Freedom of heart is found when this exchange of love happens in our inner man and our lives become ruled by desire for more of God. Even if we appear to be wonderfully successful, life is burdensome when our internal desires are not in alignment with God. Life becomes very different when our desires are touched by His grace. David Brainerd, the well-known evangelist to the Native Americans, wrote this in his diary:

Feeling somewhat of the sweetness of communion with God and the force of His love and how it captivates my soul and makes all my desires and affections to center in God, I set apart this day for fasting and prayer to God, to bless me in view of preaching the Gospel. I had life and power in prayer this afternoon. God enabled me to wrestle ardently in intercession for my friends. The Lord visited me marvelously in prayer. I think my soul was never in such agony before. I felt no restraint, for the treasures of God's grace were opened to me. I wrestled for absent friends and for the ingathering of poor souls. I was in such agony from sun half an hour high till near dark that I was all over wet with sweat. Oh! my dear Savior did sweat blood for these poor souls! I longed for more compassion toward them. I was under a sense of divine love, and went to bed in such a frame of mind, with my heart set on God.

Reward #2: Fasting enlarges our capacity for a righteous and focused life.

Through the Bridegroom fast, our desires change. God enlarges our emotions with regard to righteousness, and allows us to feel more of what He feels. He causes us to grow in a passionate zeal for righteousness and have a renewed hatred for sin. Scripture declares that Jesus loves righteousness and hates sin with a passion: "You have loved righteousness and hated lawlessness ... " (Heb. 1:9). He wants to impart this to us.

In our human nature we love sin and hate righteousness, until the grace of God turns our hearts around. God's desire for us is that we come to love what we used to hate, and hate what we used to love. When believers are casual about sin in their lives, they feel the same passivity about sin in the Church and nation at large. We do not want to get stuck in such terrible spiritual passivity. We want sin to be as repugnant to us as it is to Jesus, and we want to be gripped with His intense love for holiness. Fasting brings about this change in our emotional chemistry. We begin to be supernaturally empowered with new desires to walk in full obedience to God. It is our glory and inheritance to live cleanly and feel clean. It is a glorious gift of God to feel some of what Jesus feels about righteousness. Oh, the glory of living holy and loving it!

God not only gives us His love for righteousness, He also gives us the power and the zeal to live a focused life. We were created to live with a Holy Spirit-born intensity in our being, made to have all our energies first focused God-ward. By saying that God should be our main occupation in life, I do not mean that we should not engage in lesser things. Part of being like Him is walking in faithfulness through the routine and mundane things of life—yet in all things, directing our hearts toward the one prevailing aim of Jesus.

Jesus told Martha that only one thing was needed, and that Mary had chosen it (Luke 10:42). Mary still washed her clothes and had healthy friendships. At the same time, the banner over Mary's life was that she was a woman of one thing. Likewise, King David declared that he had only one desire: to see God's beauty (Ps. 27:4). David felt God's zeal for the things of God (Ps. 69:7-12). He was preoccupied with God as his primary source and goal of life. David gave political leadership to the nation and oversaw the military, yet he continued to be a man of one purpose. His life was focused on the Lord.

We increase in intensity, but the increase is not merely an increase in the intensity of our personality or temperament; it is an increase in our passionate focus on God. Such Spirit-born focus is a gift of God that increases as we fast. We become immovable and steady, regardless of obstacles. Those with a focused life and holy emotions can feel and act consistently whether they are promoted or demoted, when opportunities come and when they go. If our sense of success and identity as a lover of God is established, the opinions of others lose some of their power to sway our hearts. The monastic movement in Church history has traditionally called this state "detachment." I think of this holy detachment as liberty and freedom in the grace of God.

Holy Detachment from Lesser Things

As we engage in a fasted lifestyle, our problems do not all just disappear. Rather, they come into divine perspective as we begin to be preoccupied with love more than problems. As the Spirit shows us the big picture of God and eternity, we become increasingly detached from our demands for certain circumstantial ideals. Detachment is when we are no longer dominated by possessiveness, no longer living primarily before men, and we are freed from having our identity be defined by what others say of us.

The word "detachment" has a negative connotation in today's world, such as the concept of "detachment from reality." However, detachment is a desirable and holy thing when we are disengaging from a wrong focus on something other than God as the source of our joy and strength. As this detachment takes place, we respond to promotion and demotion in much the same way. We enjoy favor with men with an open hand and easily refuse promotion that distracts us from the highest things in God. Without detachment, promotion often blinds us with euphoria and we lose our ability to see it clearly as the distraction it is. When we respond to these two extremes in the same way, we experience profound freedom and a soaring spirit.

Jesus refused to allow the multitudes to promote Him to be king or president of Israel, not because it was wrong for Him to be king, but because He knew He would be King of all the kings of Earth during the Millennial Kingdom. The issue was the timing of His promotion, not whether or not He would be promoted. It was not God's will for Him to be promoted at His first coming. "When Jesus perceived that they were about to come and take Him by force to make Him king, He departed again to the mountain by Himself alone" (John 6:15). Many modern Christians would have had a difficult time turning down a good offer like that. We would automatically think of how much good we could do if we were suddenly made president of the nation. However, Jesus saw promotion differently than we do. He wanted God's perfect will more than man's affirmation of His ministry.

One of my favorite examples of this principle in Church history is seen in the life of a Catholic monk named Bernard of Clairvaux (1090-1153 AD). Bernard taught much on living a fasted lifestyle before the beauty of the Bridegroom God. This little, skinny monk was one of the most powerful men in the world during his lifetime. The kings of France, Germany and Italy respected him so much that when they got into a military conflict with one another, a simple letter from Bernard had the power to stop them. At one point in his life, the leaders in Rome wanted Bernard to be Pope, but he refused and recommended one of his disciples instead. He is the only person in history I know who refused to be Pope when asked. What reason did Bernard give for refusing? He wanted to be able to continue the same level of intimacy with God that he enjoyed at the time.

When we are pursuing the beauty of God, we do not have the same energy for vengeance or self-promotion. What bothers us or excites us changes as we move from self-centeredness to God-centeredness. Honor before men appears less powerful, vainer and more temporary. Demotion does not feel as personal and is not as devastating. Difficult circumstances are still hard, but are not as overwhelming and crippling to our lives as they once were. Our problems come into divine perspective and we begin to become preoccupied with love above all else.

Reward #3: Fasting illuminates the mind with the Spirit of Revelation.

Another of the rewards of fasting is that the Holy Spirit illuminates our understanding. Engaging in the Bridegroom fast positions us to receive revelation about the Word by sharpening our mind and enhancing the amount of revelation of God we receive. When Jesus appeared to the disciples on the Emmaus road, He opened their understanding and caused their hearts to burn within them (Luke 24:29-36). This is what we pray for as we fast—the burning Word to become alive on the inside. There is nothing more powerful than when God reveals God—when Jesus reveals Jesus—to the human heart.

Jesus said, "I have declared to them Your name, and will declare it, that the love with which you loved Me may be in them" (John 17:26). Jesus declared the name or the personality of the Father to the disciples and continues to do that today through the Holy Spirit. In doing this, He sets our hearts on fire by opening up our understanding of the Father. When Jesus reveals the Father to us, our love for God the Father grows.

Another benefit of the Bridegroom fast is that God opens up revelation to us through prophetic dreams and visions. He opens up and makes alive our understanding by giving us prophetic dreams in the night. Over the years I have experienced a marked increase of spiritual dreams and visions when I fast regularly. I believe the reason for this is that fasting sharpens our spirit to receive from God in the nighttime. It positions us to be "awake" on the inside and expecting to receive from Him. God opens His secrets to us (John 21:20).

We long to experience more of the deep and secret regions of God's heart. It's impossible to buy, earn, or manipulate our way into the inner life of God. All the money on Earth and all the power of the greatest kings could not open one window of access into the secrets of God's heart. But that which we cannot take for ourselves, we are freely given. As prayer and fasting tenderizes our spirits, we are escorted into the secret regions of His heart. The Spirit searches the deep things of God, the things that belong to Jesus, and gives them to us (1 Cor. 2:10; Ps. 25:12,14).

When the Holy Spirit does this work, we are empowered to see things about the Lord's heart that we never saw before. Many people are content to live without this type of revelation, living lives that are entrenched in spiritual boredom, and going from day to day suffocating internally. Jesus wants so much more for us. John 16:15 records Jesus saying, "All things that the Father has are Mine. Therefore I said that He will take of Mine and declare it to you."

In the process of seeing Jesus' heart, we find out what is important to Him. Through the illumination that the Holy Spirit brings, God grants divine perspective in our lives by causing the things that truly are small to seem small to us and causing the things that truly are big to seem big to us. For example, a truly small thing would be someone stealing thousands of dollars from you. This seems a big thing to us, but in reality, you would not even remember it in 500 years. It truly is small and we need to perceive it as small.

Eternity, the Second Coming of Jesus, the Great Tribulation, and the eternal fires of Hell are the truly big things of life. As big as they are, however, they usually seem remote to us and don't really capture much of our thinking. The Spirit wants to make these truths big to us. Through fasting, our understanding begins to transcend some of the common values of our culture, rising above the things that normally bog us down. We find the grace to not get lost in the pettiness that is so natural to every one of us.

Reward #4: Fasting strengthens a deep sense of our spiritual identity.

Deep within the human heart is the cry to know who we are and if we matter to someone. We long to know and feel our true identity as sons and daughters before the Father and as a Bride before the Son. The Bridegroom fast strengthens our revelation of this identity. We come into understanding of what we look like to God and begin to agree with Him in that. When we connect with our true identity in our eternal glory, we become powerful and fearless. If we know we are the kings who will rule the Earth with Jesus, then we live life very differently. "You are worthy ... for You were slain, and have redeemed us to God by Your blood ... and have made us kings and priests to our God; and we shall reign on the earth" (Rev. 5:9-10).

When we know we are Jesus' eternal companions and partners, our hearts become fiercely strong. Without this understanding, we flounder around in an unanchored spiritual life, being excessively preoccupied with ourselves. Most people are obsessed with themselves, but as we grow up we learn to restrain and cover up the expressions of our self-absorption. We learn to hide them with good manners so as to preserve our dignity before others. These cover ups, however, do not change the fact that we are enslaved to thoughts of what we look like to others. We hide it but we're still hurt when we're not recognized or noticed. It takes divine might on the inside to not be this way. The Bridegroom fast strengthens our sense of identity by weakening the lies about us that hold us captive to envy, jealousy and insecurity.

God wants us to understand who we are to Him and in Him. We were created for a kind of significance. We are designed by God to be unique and important. Our full identity is founded on the knowledge of God's affection for us. When our identity connects with our hearts we become powerful and fearless. As we fast and begin to hear the voice of the Bridegroom clearly, Jesus settles the question of who we are.

One of the most profound biblical examples of an identity being strengthened through fasting and prayer is John the Baptist. John heard the voice of the Bridegroom and it deeply touched his identity. John was a voice crying out in the wilderness. In other words, when he heard *the* Voice, he was happy to be just *a* voice instead of a famous name or face. John spent his whole life, eighteen years in the wilderness, to have only eighteen months in ministry.

Israel's response to this "greatest man ever born of a woman" was to call him demonized. "Assuredly, I say to you, among those born of women there has not risen one greater than John the Baptist ... For John came neither eating nor drinking, and they say, 'He has a demon'" (Matt. 11:11, 18). Despite this, John's heart was filled with joy at the end of his life. He lived an ascetic lifestyle and was rejected by the people, but he knew who he was. And he rejoiced.

When we hear Jesus' voice, it also changes what we want and what we fear losing. When we've heard His voice and become secure in our identity, what we fear losing most is the anointing of the Spirit on our hearts, or the power to walk in obedience before Him. The main result of knowing who we are is *fearlessness*. We have contentment in God with holy detachment from our circumstances and position. Like John, we become content to be a voice. This changed identity changes our discontentment in natural things. We become people who are living lives of another world, lives anchored in eternity.

Reward #5: Fasting equips our bodies and enhances our physical health and spiritual intimacy.

The grace given to our physical appetites during the Bridegroom fast impacts both our souls and bodies. It is common to think of intimacy with God as purely spiritual and having no relationship to our physical body, but that's not the way it works. Our bodies, souls and spirits are integrated in the design and plan of God. Our bodies are a vehicle through which we experience God, and what we do with them dynamically affects our spiritual lives. Our capacity to experience intimacy with Him is either enhanced or diminished by our physical actions. This is important to understand. God's design is brilliant. When righteousness reigns in our physical appetites, our ability to experience Him is enhanced. The opposite is also true. Although we may pursue God hard, if we fill our emotions with trash and let our physical appetites get out of rhythm with the Holy Spirit, our ability to experience His life will be quenched. This principle has three distinct applications.

Engaging in sinful physical appetites defiles our body. Our body is the temple of the Holy Spirit, and opening it up to sin is seriously damaging. Drugs, sexual immorality, excessive alcohol and gluttony are not pleasures that enhance our lives in God. The Church doesn't often talk about gluttony; the stronghold of food is rarely challenged. However, food often becomes a false god, and God's gift of grace-empowered fasting is one of the ways to dethrone it.

Overindulging in legitimate physical appetites quenches the Spirit's life in us. Lawful, God-given pleasures will dull our spirits and defile our bodies if they are allowed to reach a point of excess in our lives. It is wrong to let any pleasure become more important to us than God. Fasting from these pleasures is a good way to expose what place they have in our hearts and to keep them from becoming idols.

Neglecting God's physical health principles puts our bodies out of rhythm with the Holy Spirit. Fasting is a voluntary laying aside of strength that, paradoxically, increases the health of the normal human body. However, neglecting the God-ordained principles of physical health depletes us. Bad diets, bodies filled with toxins and poisons, poor exercise and excessive overworking without a Sabbath rest all rob us of our physical strength. Part of being wholehearted toward God is cooperating with His physical principles. Doing so gives us strength to engage in fasting and prayer.

The Physical Benefits of Fasting

Our bodies were designed to need periodic rests from food. Our digestive systems work best with this rest and our cells are given a chance to rid themselves of built-up toxins. Because we know that nutrients are necessary for our health, we logically think that not eating must be harmful. Starvation or excessive deprivation is very unhealthy, but fasting periodically and with wisdom increases our vitality. Our body exhibits its disagreement with wrong foods, or too much food, through poor health, obesity and illness.

God designed our bodies to often respond to disease with fevers and automatic fasting. We do not usually want to eat when we are sick. Fasting utilizes the God-designed healing and cleansing processes built into us. The body heals itself at the cellular level. The biochemical mechanisms of cells are complex in the way they process proteins, carbohydrates and fats. Each process produces waste that our cells must remove to avoid becoming over-filled with toxins. They need occasional rest from processing. Fasting gives them time to cleanse the toxins away. Without proper rest, our systems can become over-loaded. Fasting provides this rest.

In one study, fifty people in good health agreed to go on a three-week fast. The results showed a lowering of their cholesterol and blood pressure. In another study, fasting reduced rheumatoid arthritis and joint pain. Fasting strengthens our enzyme system, which can become overtaxed by gluttony or overindulgence. Even the medicine of ancient cultures prescribed fasting for health. Hippocrates (460-375 BC), the father of medicine, used it himself to fight illness.

The rewards of fasting before our Bridegroom God are enormous. These benefits stand in front of us as doorways beckoning our entrance. God desires that every believer partake of them, for they are truly part of basic Christianity. Along with the rewards, there are significant difficulties and even dangers in the fasted lifestyle. Just as God gives us a vision of the rewards He will give us, He also wants us to be aware of the perils as we pursue a fasted lifestyle. We will look at these difficulties and dangers in the next several chapters.

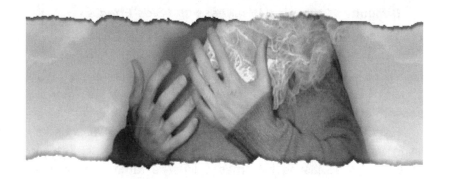

CHAPTER NINE

Seven Difficulties of the Fasted Lifestyle

Along with the benefits of the fasted lifestyle, there are very real difficulties. The rewards coexist with the burdens of fasting. Though the benefits to be experienced are truly superior, they do not invalidate or nullify the struggles we have. Over the years, we have seen people get excited about fasting and go strong for a few months, only to become disillusioned and quit. The way to sustain a lifestyle of fasting and prayer is to run at a long-distance, marathon pace. If we understand what sort of challenges may be encountered, we will be equipped with perseverance to endure them, and we will escape the disillusionment of an uninformed abandonment and unforeseen fallout. To be forewarned is to be forearmed.

The obstacles that we must be aware of are internal and external, spiritual and natural, physical and mental. Before going through these difficulties and dangers in detail, as we will in these next couple of chapters, it is important to highlight the principle that the benefits in fasting truly outweigh the burdens. Yes, there are obstacles, but the graces gained far outweigh the rigors of the obstacles if we will persevere through them.

Difficulty #1: Physical Weakness and Side Effects

The first challenge we encounter in the fasted lifestyle is physical weakness and loss of energy. When we begin to experience weakness in our natural bodies, we need not be disillusioned. This is part of embracing voluntary weakness that we might enter the strength of God.

Fasting is primarily a call to weakness; hunger is a secondary issue. Yes, we are very hungry at first, but weakness builds and accumulates as fasting becomes a lifestyle rather than just an occasional event. Even on the "eating days," we can have some physical weakness from previous "fasting days." David wrote of this: "My knees are weak through fasting, and my flesh is feeble" (Ps. 109:24).

The physical weakness encountered in fasting manifests in several different ways. First, our sleep patterns are altered in that we actually need less sleep while fasting, but the sleep we do have is irregular and not completely sound. Another manifestation of weakness we might encounter is experiencing headaches, which come about as the body detoxifies from junk foods. We can reduce this difficulty by simply changing our normal diet and eating healthier. Another normal symptom of weakness due to fasting is slight dizziness or lightheadedness when we rise too quickly. Some people experience an inner trembling and shakiness, or a wobbly, unsteady sensation. Weak legs, a weak grip and slight numbness are also all normal.

We may also experience a hypersensitivity to loud noise, touch or the activity around us. Digestion disruptions can occur in the first few months of regular fasting, until the body adjusts to this new lifestyle. Eventually, by altering our diet, we will learn to avoid the amounts and types of food that cause this difficulty. Part of fasting as a lifestyle is that even when we are not fasting, we are ordering our lives to serve the goal of strengthening this lifestyle in the strongest way possible.

Difficulty #2: Change of Metabolism

Regular fasting often causes a change of metabolism. Our metabolism is designed to slow down as a protective mechanism against starvation, when we eat less. We may lose weight during the first several months of regular fasting, but because our metabolism eventually slows down, some people end up gaining weight even though they eat less. If we fast intensely for a few years and then suddenly stop, we might not be able to immediately eat like we used to without gaining a lot of weight; it could take a year or two to speed up our metabolism to its original level.

Difficulty #3: Mental Weakness

The third challenge in the fasted lifestyle is the toll fasting takes on us mentally. We recognize this mental toll in that we are often spacey instead of clear-minded, and occasionally feel dazed, disconnected and distracted when relating to others. We become forgetful of things like people's names and the items on our to-do lists. It is sometimes harder to communicate as we struggle to find the right words. This mental weakness is definitely a burden and is sometimes even embarrassing. Yet when we remember the parallel benefit to this challenge, the illumination of our minds by divine revelation, we are reminded that it is worth it to endure this difficulty.

Difficulty #4: Emotional Stress

Part of the challenge of living the fasted lifestyle is emotional stress. This specific difficulty is a paradox in that we may experience stress in our emotions on the one hand, but on the other hand encounter tenderness in and for God. While fasting, it is normal to feel easily annoyed and irritated, often due to our hypersensitivity to noise, touch and activity. Yes, we can feel bugged by external things while feeling God's sweet presence. We can be on edge, but at the same time experience deep feelings of love for God and weep with tenderness as we read the Word. It is common to feel periods of heaviness while fasting. But even when we feel "down," we experience intimacy with Jesus.

Fasting temporarily minimizes our strength in our natural emotions. By nature, we hide and cover up our emotional weakness by the strength of our personalities. The weakness in our souls can be hidden like fault lines just beneath the Earth's surface. We can cover the emotions of fear, anger, impatience, rejection, depression, sorrow, and other emotions. We can temporarily keep ourselves in line and act properly with the edge-reducer of food.

Fasting, however, minimizes some of the natural strength we use to suppress our weak spots. The props that anesthetize our pain are taken away, and our raw weakness stares us in the face. We may feel like hypocrites when this happens, but the truth is that we are deeper in God than before. The weakness we have hidden is now glaringly clear. It was always there and was clear to God. Now it is clear to us as well. By revealing the truth of these hidden fault lines in our personalities, we have the opportunity to walk into a new freedom. As we learn to continually bring these fault lines to God, we are transformed, humbled and taught how to walk in the freedom of weakness.

Difficulty #5: Loss of Effectiveness in the Short Term

Another stumbling block that we must be aware of as we give ourselves to the fasted lifestyle is that we may undergo a weakened resolve to work and feel unmotivated to get things done. When people fast consistently, they cannot be as focused because of mental weakness, they cannot work as hard because of physical weakness, and they cannot produce as effectively as they could if they were not fasting because of their loss of resolve to accomplish things in the natural. Because of the loss of energy and attentiveness that attends frequent fasting, it is common to be less effective in our ministry and business. In other words, our success before man may seem to diminish somewhat during periods of fasting. Though this loss of effectiveness in the short term is real and taxing, we find a strengthened resolve in our relationship with God.

Barring health issues or pregnancy, everyone can fast two days a week without negative side effects on our health. Yes, our performance in study and work may be mildly affected. We accept that we will get less done in the short run, but know that in God's economy we will produce far more with renewed spiritual vitality. In the long run, our effectiveness is significantly greater because God's favor and activity are released in the midst of our weakened labors.

The Western mindset measures productivity differently than God does. In the Kingdom of God, there is often a delay factor as we wait for the Lord's blessing on what we do. Some of the great saints seemed ineffective during their ministries. For example, Anna's true greatness could not be seen during her lifetime, but she helped prepare the atmosphere for the Messiah's coming. John the Baptist spent possibly eighteen years in a fasted lifestyle for only eighteen months of visible ministry, yet God called John the greatest man born of a woman. Mary of Bethany's extravagance of devotion was considered a waste on the Earth, but Jesus declared her life to be a memorial remembered forever by all.

Difficulty #6: Relational Disruptions and Social Pressures

We do not lead solitary lives. Therefore, as we give ourselves to the fasted lifestyle, the impact will not only be felt personally, but will affect our relationships and perhaps even create tension in some relationships. The challenge is heightened by the fact that the values of Western culture are opposed to the fasted lifestyle. Because of this, conflict is sure to eventually arise.

I have had many conversations where people urged me to play more and pray less so that I might live a more "balanced" life as they do. People want you to be happy with what makes them happy. When you're happy with something else, they sometimes feel rejected or judged by you. People often feel judged by the lifestyles of those who do not have the same desire for possessions, comforts and pleasures. They think you are "off" because of the amount of fasting and prayer that you do. They insist that you need more socializing and entertainment to keep you from getting too far "out there." The multitudes called John the Baptist demonized (Matt. 11:18).

David's friends and brothers considered him "off" because of his zeal for God. David said that it was for God's sake he bore this reproach with them. This tension grew to such a degree that David became like a stranger to his brothers. The elders and leaders spoke against him and the drunkards sang songs mocking him as a religious fanatic. David told us that all this happened because zeal for God's house consumed him. When he wept and chastened his soul with fasting, his actions became a reason for others to reproach or criticize him (Ps. 69:7-12).

Fasting makes us more fearless in our spirits. This can cause relational problems as well. Fearless, anointed, lovesick worshippers do not care so much about being promoted or demoted, or about running in the rat race for man's favor. People with this type of confidence can cause some disturbance by making social and economic choices and speaking boldly on issues. Those who walk in the fasted lifestyle are free from false comforts in their quest for that which is eternal. Fearlessness annoys and even angers those who are building their lives upon temporal foundations. This can take a relational toll with those who want to see us dial things down to live like they do. It will unsettle some who want you to desire the temporal things that they desire.

The lovesick are often accused of being elitist, socially isolated or super spiritual because they do not want to socialize in the same way they did before embracing the fasted lifestyle. They do socialize, but not in the same way as they did before. That is the key distinction. True fellowship is actually hindered by the way many Christians hang out and "socialize." Much of it involves significant amounts of wasted time without real spiritual encouragement or servanthood, which communicate God's heart to others. Col.4:6 says, "Let your speech always be with grace, seasoned with salt."

Eph. 4:29 says, "Let no corrupt word proceed out of your mouth, but what is good for necessary edification, that it may impart grace to the hearers."

People may call their socializing fellowship, but much of it is no more than idle chatter, vain babbling, and coarse jesting (Eph. 5:4), filled with inappropriate amounts of what I call sitcom humor. "All uncleanness or covetousness, let it not even be named among you, as is fitting for saints; neither filthiness, nor foolish talking, nor coarse jesting, which are not fitting, but rather giving of thanks" (Eph. 5:3-4). What is commonly called fellowship is not true fellowship. True fellowship requires sharing God's life and revelation with one another (1 John 1:1-5). To fellowship in the way the Bible describes, people must pursue pure lives with holy speech and have vibrant spirits in the Word.

We must not walk in complete isolation, have spiritual pride, or judge others who do not fast. Yet, we must take ample time to be in the Word and in prayer. There is absolutely no substitute for time with God. Walking this out in the midst of a Church culture that does not value spending time with God is difficult. How to do this is an imperfect science. We all have much to learn in this, but we must not draw back from the tensions of embracing this lifestyle because of the fear of man. Remember, we are not running a popularity contest but seeking to walk in holy love. We must have a vibrant life in God to do this. We answer to the Lord on the last day of this life, not to the socialites in our church who do not understand us.

Difficulty #7: An Increase of Demonic Attack

The final difficulty of the fasted lifestyle that we will consider in this chapter is that demonic attacks often increase against those seeking to walk in the fullness of God. As the Holy Spirit increases His activity in us, the devil increases his attack against us. The enemy specifically targets the lifestyle that releases God's power.

Anthony of Egypt was the first well known monk in Christian history. He obeyed the Lord with intense fasting and prayer for twenty years. After twenty years, at age forty-five, the Lord began using him to perform powerful signs and wonders. This lasted for the next sixty years, until he died at age 106. He experienced terrifying encounters with demons who threatened to physically torment him if he did not stop fasting.

It is common for those who fast and pray with unusual intensity to tell of experiences where demons manifested to threaten and to strike fear into them. In these attacks we must stay in relationship with like-minded believers and read God's Word often. The paradox is that fasting draws more demonic attacks, but is one of the things the Spirit uses to help us *overcome* the attacks of the enemy. We need not waver at such times, because He who is in us is greater than he who is in the world (1 John 4:4).

It is wise to be aware of the potential difficulties we might experience as we enter into a life of fasting and prayer. By acknowledging them and being warned of them, we are freed to embrace the benefits and rewards of fasting in their fullness. These difficulties are not meant as discouragements, but exhortations. As Jesus said, we who desire to follow Him must first count the cost (Luke 14:28). In the next chapter, we will address seven potential pitfalls that the lovesick warrior must be prepared to avoid.

CHAPTER TEN

Seven Dangers of the Fasted Lifestyle

Fasting has glorious benefits, but It can be like swimming in shark-infested waters, as the enemy, Satan, lurks in the deep, seeking to devour us. We have considered some of the difficulties of the fasted lifestyle; now let us consider some of the dangers.

Fasting is not neutral in its effects upon our lives. It strengthens us for good, or it contributes to drawing us off the path of biblical wisdom and righteousness. Whatever motivation we have when fasting, that is what is *strengthened* in us. This is what we mean by saying that fasting is not neutral. If our motivation is to grow in love, then this is what will be strengthened in us. On the other hand, if our motives are for self-exaltation, then negative things will be strengthened in us as we fast. Thus, it is important that we not treat fasting casually, with unchecked motives, or we will be at risk of doing more harm than good to our spiritual lives.

The pursuit of wholeheartedness has potential dangers related to it. We need to use wisdom and not be simplistic or naïve, knowing there are such dangers as the possibility of counterfeit demonic encounters, isolationism, a spirit of poverty, eating disorders, legalism that operates in a religious spirit (seeking to earn our standing with God), inappropriate asceticism, and spiritual pride. The only way we can be safe from falling into these is by pursuing 100-percent obedience as we stay committed to other believers, and by spending much time in the Word of God. Scripture is the final authority that judges all our experiences.

Danger #1: Demonic Deceptions and Doctrines

"For such are false apostles, deceitful workers, transforming themselves into apostles of Christ. And no wonder! For Satan himself transforms himself into an angel of light" (2 Cor. 11:13-14). Fasting, like dynamite, has great power that can be used for either good or evil. Whether this activity is used for good purposes or bad, the results in the soul are always powerful and never neutral. This is a point of utmost importance because the enemy wants us to be swayed into darkness without realizing it.

Fasting sensitizes the human spirit to the spirit realm, including both the genuine and the occult realms. Many false religions and occult groups promote the practice of fasting because they know it releases power. They are often led by people committed to fasting who deny their flesh to have a greater access to the spirit realm. Many of the major false religions on Earth were started by those who were engaged in extreme seasons of prayer and fasting. Those in Eastern religions are often much more committed to fasting than those in the western Church.

Satan counterfeits the things of God in an attempt to deceive the faithful. Even believers can receive demonic visions that lead them into delusions of grandeur. Christians who increase their fasting may experience an increase of demonic activity designed to confuse and deceive them. When people fast intensely, Satan may attack by giving them supernatural experiences that lead them into false doctrine. This is not unusual or unexpected.

Demonic deception will increase to unprecedented levels before Jesus returns. Paul prophesied that in the End-Times some would fall away from Christianity because they paid attention to demons.

"Now the Spirit expressly says that in the latter times some will depart from the faith, giving heed to deceiving spirits and doctrines of demons" (1 Tim. 4:1).

Recognizing this real danger, we must warn sincere believers who love Jesus and who go on long fasts, but who do not have a strong foundation in the Word. They can be deceived with delusional ideas about themselves. To give an example of this, years ago, one of our dedicated intercessors retreated into the woods to go on a long fast. He came back convinced that he would single-handedly stop abortion in America. He had grandiose ideas about himself as the one who would save America and be the main person to change history. He continued to go to prayer meetings for several years but then began isolating himself, not reading his Bible, and indulging in long fasts. After a few years, he fell away from the faith.

I have met people who, after engaging in long fasts, believed they were Elijah or one of the Two Witnesses described in Revelation, or an especially anointed one ordained to fight the Antichrist. The stories are endless of sincere believers who get deceived by approaching fasting in an unwise or inappropriate way. They believe false ideas about their superior spirituality and calling. This is a clear and present danger, especially in this time of history.

The common trend among these deceived people is that they embrace intensive fasting, separate themselves from other believers, and neglect the Word. We must be on special guard during times of fasting, and make a special effort to stay focused on intimacy with Jesus, connected to the Body of Christ in authentic relationship, immersed in the Word of God, even twice as much as usual, and open to correction from those in spiritual authority.

If we allow ourselves to become isolated from people and neglect to read the Word, we will lose our focus on intimacy and we may find ourselves seeking that which leads to our own spiritual grandeur. The fruit of the true Bridegroom fast is hearts that are becoming more humble, submissive and tender, rather than increasing in pride and growing distant from others.

Danger #2: Isolationism

One of the common dangers of fasting is isolationism. Those who regularly fast can easily lose their way when they become isolated from the Body of Christ. Fasting must be accompanied by great humility and godly interdependence on one another in order to preserve us from wrong thinking. God has set up His Kingdom in such a way that we must pursue the Lord together as a family. We are not complete in ourselves. We are only complete when we're functioning together as the Body of Christ (Col. 2:10; 1 Cor. 12:12-25). We have the mind of Christ (1 Cor. 2:16) as we relate to one another. This cannot and does not happen in isolation. Notice Paul said that "we" together have the mind of Christ. He did not say "I" have it in my isolation.

When entering a lifestyle of fasting and prayer, we must be intentional about being committed to our brothers and sisters in the Lord. Isolationism disregards the glory and grace of God that is imparted to others. It is anti-servanthood, anti-compassion and anti-social—all realities that stand in opposition to the heart of God. Some historical monastic movements focused on being free from personal defilement and fell into the error of isolationism. They shunned being involved with other people because they imagined it meant they would be exposed to potential defilement.

However, Scripture calls us to the fasted lifestyle because it is the best way to fulfill the two great commandments—loving God and loving others. Jesus even said that our greatness was measured by serving one another (Matt. 20:26-28; Luke 22:26). It is true that we absolutely must have times alone with God, and that we each maintain our own personal pursuit of intimacy with God. But it is essential to stay committed to other believers; we must refuse to retreat into a strange isolation.

Danger #3: A Spirit of Poverty

Another pitfall to avoid in the fasted lifestyle is that, in our quest to live simply, we must not allow ourselves to fall prey to a spirit of material poverty. The spirit of material poverty deludes people into believing they must give everything away because having abundance is wrong—or because having nothing will stop covetousness. It's true that one of the prevailing problems in the western Church is the spirit of covetousness. The answer to this common error is not a spirit of poverty, but rather a generous spirit that gives to others in an extravagant way. One of the great perils of a spirit of poverty is pride in self-abasement that judges others who refuse to embrace this wrong spirit. We need to understand that prosperity is a blessing of the Lord. He promises to supply all of our needs (Deut. 8:18; Luke 6:38; 2 Cor. 8-9; Phil. 4:19; 3 John 2). Because we want to be rich in blessing and give to others, we are to resist the spirit of poverty and believe God for financial increase (1 Tim. 6:17-19). Yes, we will receive much increase, and yes, we will give it away freely. Why would we rejoice in lack? We rejoice that we can share abundantly with others as we pursue a deep spirituality.

Danger #4: Eating Disorders

Another danger zone in fasting that must be avoided is the temptation to fast out of wrong motivations that flow from eating disorders. Eating disorders are a serious problem and are at an all-time high in our culture today among Christians and non-Christians alike. Be aware that a person might begin fasting with pure motivations and slowly move into false motivations without being aware of it. They become empowered by thinking they are responding to the biblical exhortations to fast, but the result is that they are strengthened in their resolve to continue in their eating disorder.

Eating disorders are very dangerous and are rooted in darkness. Anyone who has struggled with one knows that fasting can be a serious trap. We fast to position our hearts to receive more from the Lord, not to enhance our appearance. We must not seek our identity in being thin but in being loved by God. I urge people to watch over those in their midst who may be prone to this. Satan wants to kill, steal and destroy human life (John 10:10) by any means possible. If he cannot destroy us by overindulgence, then he will go to the other extreme and try to trick us into denying our flesh for wrong reasons.

Danger #5: Legalism and the Religious Spirit

Another common danger in fasting is becoming ensnared in legalism. Legalism, also called a religious spirit, seeks to earn one's standing with God by dedication and personal effort. The Pharisees were driven by a legalistic spirit. They fasted to earn something from God. They boasted and judged the people who didn't fast as they did. The spirit of legalism opposes the spirit of grace. Our motivation in fasting should have everything to do with responding to God's love. It is not fasting to gain standing with God through our works, but rather to enter more deeply into the experience of His freely-given love.

It is best when we fast out of the place of marveling over the free grace He shows us. It's not fasting to earn or deserve, but rather to have a greater capacity to live in agreement with the Holy Spirit, whom we love. Anyone who is not grounded in the grace of God should wait before they start fasting in more aggressive ways. Otherwise, legalism may be strengthened in them as they fast. The foundation for fasting that doesn't degenerate into legalism is the knowledge that God embraces us with delight, even in our weakness.

Paul addressed the problem of legalism in the book of Galatians. He warned these saints not to accept the religious spirit. "O foolish Galatians! Who has bewitched you ... ? Did you receive the Spirit by the works of the law, or by the hearing of faith? Are you so foolish? Having begun in the Spirit, are you now being made perfect by the flesh?" (Gal. 3:1-3). He went on to exhort them to stand fast in the liberty by which Christ has made us free by His glorious work on the cross, and to not be entangled with a yoke of religious bondage called legalism. Legalism would cause them to be estranged from

Christ, for they would fall from grace if they attempted to stand before God based on their good works and dedication (Gal. 5:1-8).

How do we know if we are operating in a spirit of legalism or a religious spirit? Let's ask ourselves a few questions. Do we feel more confident before God and worship with greater assurance because we are fasting? Do we tend to shrink back in shame when we are not fasting? If so, we know we are putting confidence in our fasting or in our dedication to God rather than His dedication to us. This is a deceptive trap, which leads to one of two dead ends: condemnation or pride.

If people in this deception do not fast, they end up in condemnation, thinking that God is disappointed with them. When they do fast, they fall into spiritual pride, imagining that God is now pleased with them based on their asceticism. The religious spirit of self-loathing that condemns us when we do not fast is the same spirit that boasts in us when we follow through in our fasting and prayer, and both find their roots in spiritual pride. Beloved, we must never think that God's affections for us are greater because we are fasting. We don't fast to make Him like us; we fast because we understand that He already likes us. Our confidence before Him should be grounded in Jesus' work on the cross (2 Cor. 5:17-21; Phil. 3:4-9) and the truth of His love for us.

If we think that we are more desirable to God because of our prayer and fasting, we are on the road to dead religion. Paul warned the early Church against the spiritual deception and pride that can come with self-denial. Some in the city of Colosse based their confidence before God on their religious rigors. They kept rules of "Do not taste, touch or handle" (Col. 2:21). Paul said, in essence, "Why do you subject yourselves to your own regulations and rules that you created, finding confidence in these lists?" (Col. 2:20). He wrote in Col. 2:23, "These things indeed have an appearance of wisdom, in self-imposed religion, false humility and neglect of the body, but are of no value against the indulgence in the flesh." He exposed their false humility and self-promotion. We must beware of *magnifying* ourselves in the act of *denying* ourselves. It is a grave danger.

All of God's children can enter into the free enjoyment of God, regardless of whether we have fasted that week. The knowledge that a tender Bridegroom cherishes us fuels our desire to be fully surrendered to the Lord. People who fast before what they perceive to be an angry God are desperately scrambling to avoid the disapproval of the Judge. If we view God this way, we end up condemning ourselves most of the time, and missing the affection and tenderness of God in our fasting. It is only in the presence of a Bridegroom of joy that our fasting is safe and most edifying to us.

A religious spirit does not enhance our gratitude or our affection for God and others. Rather, it compares itself with others and boasts in its greater commitment. It puts a false dividing line between the "spiritual" and "unspiritual," creating discord and disunity. If we are fasting because of love, there is no boasting or comparison. There is no competition. There is only the desire to love God and receive love from God, and to bring others into this marvelous experience of God's affections.

Danger #6: Inappropriate Asceticism or Self-Denial

We must watch for two great enemies of fasting: the destructiveness of carnal self-indulgence and the destructiveness of religious self-denial. Though there are more perils in self-indulgence than in abstinence, the dangers of fasting come when our focus is not on a God of love, a God of burning affections. The Bridegroom fast leads us into having confidence in God's burning heart of love, not in our flesh. It leads us into an essential deliverance from ungodly self-denial.

Jesus calls us to take up our cross and deny ourselves as we follow Him in the grace of God (Matt. 16:24-25). False asceticism leads people into confidence in their religious sufferings instead of God's mercy and goodness. The enemy seeks to pervert this glorious pathway of obedience and derail anyone who takes it seriously, deceiving them into extremes that are not prescribed by Scripture.

Some monasteries in the Dark Ages entered into strange kinds of asceticism—beating themselves with whips and wearing painful clothing or objects. Paul speaks of the false ascetics making celibacy mandatory and imposing dietary restrictions.

Throughout Church history, people have tried tortuous regimes of self-denial in an attempt to keep themselves from immorality and indulgence of the flesh. These extremes are rooted in false assumptions about God and how His grace operates. They are not biblical and will not lead us to encounter the heart of Jesus. What keeps our hearts in holiness is revelation of the love and beauty of God. We are seated with Christ in heavenly places (Eph. 2:6). Therefore, we have access to God's presence and thus, to the beauty of His majesty. Fasting is about having confidence in grace. It is not about marking off religious to do lists or how severely "spiritual" we can be. It is the strength of God's love that seals and empowers our hearts, not the strength of our own flesh (Song 8:6).

Danger #7: Spiritual Pride

The premier pitfall in the fasted lifestyle is the fierce temptation toward spiritual pride. Abstinence from food and pleasure can greatly stoke our pride. This pride is the most common danger of the fasted lifestyle, and it is lethal to true spiritually. There is nothing more powerful than a group of people united in abandonment to God, praying and fasting together. However, such a community has a corresponding great and continual temptation to pride and judgmentalism.

The call to the fasted lifestyle is a premier opportunity for elitism—hidden feelings of superiority—to manifest in our lives. Prideful elitism and self-congratulations for spiritual achievement are among the most common manifestations of spiritual pride. At IHOP-KC, we ask that all abide by our corporate fasting principle of "don't ask, don't tell" related to the details of what they do in times of corporate fasts. It is easy to feel superior to others in fasting. Jesus warned us of this when He said, "When you fast, do not be like the hypocrites, with a sad countenance. For they disfigure their faces that they may appear to men to be fasting" (Matt. 6:16).

What does spiritual pride look like? We find ourselves desiring to be recognized as one uniquely dedicated and close to God. We love being acknowledged as one who fasts. We feel gratification when we get "caught" fasting. We are disgusted that others aren't fasting as much as we are. We feel superior or judgmental toward those who don't fast. I know about this because I have often walked in this spiritual pride. It grieves me whenever I glimpse pride in my heart. By nature, we are desperate to appear closer to God than others, even if it requires us to give off exaggerated and false impressions about the depth of our spirituality. We want others to believe more about us than what is actually true. Though we may hear all of these manifestations of spiritual pride and quickly decide they do not apply to us, we must remember just how subtle pride is, and be always on the lookout for its residue in our motivations and mindsets. It may be more personal to us than we realize. This is the main struggle for sincere people.

Another face of spiritual pride is having an unholy confidence in judging people. Fasting provides a tremendous open door for religious arrogance. Without a purposeful resistance to pride, we will unknowingly begin to judge others. In light of this, Paul urged, "Therefore let us not judge one another anymore, but rather resolve this, not to put a stumbling block or a cause to fall in our brother's way" (Rom. 14:13).

Sometimes those who have given themselves to intense prayer and fasting are the most angry and judgmental people. Who killed the Messiah? Pharisees who fasted twice a week (Luke 18:12). They were emboldened to judge others by their religious deception and pride. Instead of looking down at others with contempt, the Lord wants us to grow in gratitude for the grace working in our hearts that enables us to sustain a fasted lifestyle. Jesus told a parable about two men who went to the temple to pray, one a Pharisee and the other a tax collector. The Pharisee thanked God that he was not like other men, noting that he fasted twice a week and gave tithes of all he possessed. The tax collector cried out, "God be merciful to me, a sinner!" He was the one justified, not the Pharisee (Luke 18:10-14).

Jesus called His people to night and day prayer in Luke 18:1-8. "Shall God not avenge His own elect who cry out day and night to Him" (Luke 18:7). When I was 23 years old, the Lord used this passage to call me to a life of intercession. I went from spending zero time in intercession to spending large amounts of time in it. However, spiritual tragedy struck my prayer life within a year. I could have avoided it if I had understood the very next paragraph in Luke 18, where Jesus warned against the pride that the Pharisees had in their regular prayer and fasting (Luke 18:9-14). I did not see that warning until it was too late.

When I began to seek to live a life of prayer, I did not realize that I would need so much of the grace of God to sustain it. I was disgusted with others who were not praying as much as I was for revival in St. Louis, where I lived at that time, and I was vocal about my anger. Then the Lord lifted the grace for prayer off my life. At that point, I was in a difficult place. I was a spiritually proud 24-year-old who had publicly announced that I was committed to leading prayer meetings several hours a day. It was horrible to lead them without any grace on my heart.

I began to hate going to my own prayer meetings, but I couldn't quit attending because of my pride. I had made such a show out of calling everyone to long hours of prayer. I continued to go even though I hated every minute. I felt oppressed. When fasting, I could not make it past noon without eating. Finally, the Lord let me know that I had grieved the Holy Spirit so much that He would not help me in prayer until I confessed my spiritual pride to others and humbled myself. I reluctantly did this. Though it was a horrible time in my life, afterwards the grace for prayer returned.

Since then I have been more aware of the extent of help I need to pray. I still lose sight of this sometimes, but by God's mercy He continues to call me to repent. I am grateful to God for helping me to somewhat sustain prayer and fasting over the years, instead of being so angry with those who do not have this grace. Now I know that the very desire to fast and pray is a work of grace and is not from our own personal, superior dedication.

When God gives the revelation of the importance of prayer with fasting and then gives us the grace to sustain it, the only response is to say, "Thank You, Lord, for this glorious gift." When gratitude for grace arises in our hearts, the dragon of pride is held somewhat in check. To those who have received this way of life, I say that it is not mostly because they are superior followers of Jesus, but rather because He is an excellent leader. It is not that we are good students; it is that Jesus is an excellent teacher. It has never been about our ability to listen all that well, but about His exceptional ability to communicate in a way that gets our attention.

As we humble ourselves and receive the revelation that God's grace is the only reason we can obey Him in any capacity, we are in a good position to resist the devil's schemes against the fasted lifestyle. Sincere believers who love Jesus and want to enter the fasted lifestyle must develop a strong foundation in what the Word says about the grace of God. During times of fasting, we must stay focused on intimacy with Jesus; stay connected to the Body of Christ in authentic relationship; stay in the Word, even twice as much as usual; and continue in humility of spirit, easily receiving correction from those in spiritual authority. We will thus avoid the seven dangers of the fasted lifestyle and move forward into the abounding benefits and rewards God desires to bring forth in our lives.

CHAPTER ELEVEN

How to Respond to Global Crisis

The Dynamics of Prayer

God has given the human race great dignity by giving us free will, which means we have been given the ability to make real decisions that have both temporal and eternal consequences. While the nobility of choice can be glorious if exercised in righteousness, it can also be perilous if swayed by sin and rebellion. A failure to soberly recognize the response the Word of God necessitates will result in a life of squandered opportunities

However, the wisdom of a lifestyle of obedience to the precepts of Scripture will have dramatic impact on our lives in this age, and will be forever rewarded in the age to come. One of the wisest choices that we can make in this life is to pray. Prayer can be expressed in many edifying forms, ranging from quiet devotional meditation to corporate intercessory prayer for revival. In this context we will focus on the function of *intercessory prayer.*

Ps. 2 reveals an astounding facet of the relationship between the Father and the Son, bestowing significance to prayer that we can scarcely fathom. In verse 8, God the Father says to the Jesus the Son, "Ask of Me, and I will give you the nations for Your inheritance, and the ends of the earth for Your possession." Peering into the mystery of the Godhead, we see that the Man Jesus, as the second Person of the Trinity, operates His government through *intercession.* Throughout His days on Earth, He was ever retreating in seclusion to pray (Mark 1:35; Luke 5:16). Jesus chose the apostles after a night in prayer (Luke 6:12), and in the hours leading up to His crucifixion He cried out to God on behalf of His disciples (John 17). Jesus' role in prayer stretches far beyond the bounds of His first coming. He sits at the right hand of God and ever lives to make intercession (Rom. 8:34; Heb. 7:25). When He returns and rules the Earth from Zion, His government will function as a house of prayer for all nations (Isaiah 56:7).

These are only glimpses into the majestic truth woven throughout Scripture: that prayer is the primary mode God has chosen for Jesus to release the Father's power and usher in His everlasting Kingdom. As His Bride, when we pray, we are entering into partnership with Him, the eternal intercessor. As Christ sought friends to watch with Him in the Garden of Gethsemane (Mark 14:32-38), forever He invites His people into the intimacy and authority of prayer.

Our decision to embrace this invitation or to neglect it has profound ramifications. Regardless of what people or demons do, God will accomplish the main events of the plan He has determined for the future—such as Jesus' Second Coming, His reign over the whole Earth as King, Satan being cast into the Lake of Fire, et cetera. However, He has given us a dynamic role, through our response to Him in prayer, fasting and obedience, in determining some of the "quality of life" we experience in the natural and in the spiritual. He opens doors of blessing and closes doors of oppression in response to our prayers. There are blessings God will only release as His people ask for them in the intimate partnership of prayer. There are demonic oppressions that only leave as a result of prayer and fasting (Matt.17:21). Isaiah taught that He longs to release His grace and power, but actually waits until He hears the cry of His people in intercession. "The Lord longs to be gracious to you, and therefore He waits on High to have compassion on you ... .He will surely be gracious to you at the sound of your cry; when He hears it, He will answer you" (Is. 30:18-19, NAS).

Corporate Intercessory Worship

All manner of prayer is important, but the highest expression of the authority the redeemed can enjoy is found in *corporate intercessory worship.* It is important to understand each of these three components and why they are so significant.

Corporate

It requires humility to embrace all that is implied in gathering corporately. Differences in worship and prayer styles, doctrinal emphases, and our personalities make humility necessary if we are to gather together in a regular way. The meekness this engenders in our hearts fosters an atmosphere conducive to the activity of the Holy Spirit. The Book of Acts again and again depicts the apostolic company of believers as united together in prayer in conjunction with the great release of the power of the Holy Spirit (Acts 1:14; 2:1; 4:24; 5:12). There are many other Scriptures that communicate this truth as well. For example, David said, "Behold, how good and how pleasant it is for brethren to dwell together in unity! ... For there the Lord commanded the blessing" (Ps. 133:1,3). Acts 1:14 is another example: "These all continued with one accord in prayer and supplication ... "

The Father only releases His fullness to His family. We can go only so far in God in our individual dedication; there is a ceiling in the Spirit until we come together. It takes a corporate, unified response over a period of time to reach the highest levels of God's intended blessing over a city or nation. Also, the fire in our hearts can die out when we are alone. We are strengthened by clustering together with people of similar passion and vision.

Intercessory

Intercessory prayer cries out to God on behalf of others and influences the courses of nations. Ezekiel expressed God's desire for one who would stand in the gap between Himself and Israel, someone who would pray in a way that would cause God's judgment to be withheld. Finding no intercessor, the Lord destroyed the land. "So I sought for a man among them who would make a wall, and stand in the gap before Me on behalf of the land, that I should not destroy it; but I found no one" (Ezek. 22:30). When God was angry with Israel because of her sin, Moses stood in the gap between Israel and God in prayer. God actually relented, or changed His plan, and did not destroy the nation. Moses' intercession resulted in God manifesting His mercy instead of judgment (Ex. 32:9-14).

It is not enough for us to only pray to express our personal devotion to God. Many who love their communion with God in prayer do not have revelation of the authority the Church has in intercession. We are called to stand with authority in the gap for others, whether for the Church, for whole cities and nations, or for individuals who do not yet know the Lord.

Worship

Finally, when corporate intercession occurs in the setting of prophetic music and songs, it unifies, sustains, and inspires God's people in a unique way. More people can enter in at a deeper level for longer periods of time when prayer is coupled with anointed worship. In Rev. 5:8, the elders who are gathered around the throne hold a harp, which represents worship, and a bowl, which represents the prayers of the saints. To join worship and intercession is in accordance with the eternal pattern of Heaven.

The importance of grasping the power of corporate intercessory worship is dramatically heightened in our day because the Earth stands upon the brink of unprecedented calamity and revival. A storm of glory and judgment looms on the horizon, and we must have discernment concerning the appropriate response to the Day that will come as a snare on all those who dwell in the nations (Luke 21:35). God's primary call to a nation in crisis is to gather together to pray, worship, fast and repent of our sins, asking God to release His power on our behalf. Yet before looking more closely at the response God beckons from us, we must better understand the nature of the imminent world-wide upheaval.

Understanding Global Crisis

Joel 2:11 says, "For the day of the Lord is great and very terrible; who can endure it?" Matt. 24:21 says, "For then there will be great tribulation, such as has not been since the beginning of the world until this time, no, nor ever shall be."

Jesus spoke of a generation that would endure tribulation unlike any other time In history. Beginning with Enoch, who lived long before Abraham and Moses, God began to give revelation of this future Day (Jude 14-15). From the Psalms to the Major and Minor Prophets, to the New Testament, including the Book of Revelation, there is more information concerning this time in history than any other time frame. Yet today much of the Body of Christ is unacquainted with the truths God has unfolded related to this time frame. Most believers live as though it will never come.

Although it is beyond the scope of this chapter to delve into the Scriptural details of the period leading up to the Second Coming, it is helpful to identify four specific sources, which overlap to produce widespread crisis on the Earth: God's zeal for righteousness as expressed through His temporal judgments, Satan's rage, man's sin and creation's groan. These factors work together under God's sovereignty and wisdom.

God's Zeal

God's judgments are motivated by His zeal for purity in His people. The Church is quick to talk about Satan's role, and even sinful man's role, but we are hesitant and uncertain about God's role in causing crisis. God's role is to oppose every operation of His enemy, which is sin. Even the chosen nation, Israel, made herself God's enemy by living in sin: "But they rebelled and grieved His Holy Spirit; so He turned Himself against them as an enemy, and

He fought against them" (Is. 63:10). Agreement with darkness, even when practiced by those who know Jesus, results in an adversarial relationship with the Holy One of Israel. James 4:4 is clear about this: "Adulterers and adulteresses! Do you not know that friendship with the world is enmity with God? Whoever wants to be a friend of the world makes himself an enemy of God."

It is clearly the Lamb of God who is the One opening the seals and orchestrating the events described in the Book of Revelation. Yet God's role in judgment is very controversial, even within the Church. His purpose in judgment is to remove everything that hinders love. He takes no pleasure in pouring out His judgment on the wicked (Ezek. 33:11). He will destroy sin's tyranny over the kingdoms of the world and establish a Kingdom of righteousness that will never end (Rev. 11:15). He will dispense wrath upon the wicked and He will discipline those in the Church who are in rebellion in order to bring them into purity. When Jesus splits the sky at His Second Coming and descends with a shout (1 Thess. 4:16), He will forcibly remove all things that offend, and He will have a Bride who is spotless (Matt. 13:41; Rev. 19:7-8).

Satan's Rage

Satan's rage causes great turmoil on the Earth within the boundaries that God sets. As the hour of his condemnation becomes imminent, Satan will unleash his fury against the nation of Israel and all those who follow the Lamb, as described in Rev.12:12, which says, "Woe to the inhabitants of the earth and the sea! For the devil has come down to you, having great wrath, because he knows that he has a short time."

Man's Sin

The most terrifying problem that a nation in sin will face is God. This is a far more threatening problem than Satan's attacks, natural disasters, or the plots of terrorists. Men can use their free wills to harm one another. They are responsible for the wars and acts of violence that are multiplying in these days.

Creation's Groans and Travails

We see this manifested in earthquakes, violent weather patterns and more. There is a mysterious but glorious connection between the actions of the human race and the condition of the natural creation, such as land and vegetation. When Adam sinned, a curse came upon the land (Gen. 3:17-18). That curse has been escalating as man's sin escalates. The Earth's convulsions will increase as sin ripens (Is. 24:19-20).

The Response that God Requires

God is calling the entire human race to repentance. It is particularly important, however, to have clarity regarding the Church's response, because we are the first line of defense in the day of shaking. God said, "If My people who are called by My name will humble themselves, and pray and seek My face, and turn from their wicked ways, then I will hear from heaven, and will forgive their sin and heal their land" (2 Chr. 7:14). Peter also expressed this in 1 Peter 4:16-18: "For the time has come for judgment to begin at the house of God; and if it begins with us first, what will be the end of those who do not obey the gospel of God?" (verse 17).

The Church, as the covenant people in the land, is most responsible before Heaven to cry out, stand in the gap and oppose sin. Furthermore, in the midst of the End Times, the condition of the nations will rapidly degenerate into chaos. As famine, pestilence, deception and conflict all escalate, multitudes will be stricken with fear, confusion and rage. In this tumult of despair and depravity, the redeemed must arise. With hearts emboldened by confidence in the Word of God and full of love for Jesus, we will lead the groping throngs to the truth of the Gospel.

> *"Now, therefore," says the Lord, "turn to Me with all your heart, with fasting, with weeping, and with mourning." So rend your heart, and not your garments; return to the Lord your God, for He is gracious and merciful, slow to anger,*

and of great kindness; and He relents from doing harm.
Who knows if He will turn and relent, and leave a blessing
behind Him ... ? Blow the trumpet in Zion, consecrate a
fast, call a sacred assembly; gather the people, sanctify the
congregation, assemble the elders, gather the children and
nursing babes ... Let the priests ... weep between the porch
and the altar; let them say, "Spare Your people, O Lord ..."
(Joel 2:12-17).

During crisis God requires a specific response from His people.
In Joel 2:12-17, God tells us exactly what we are to do to receive
His mercy and deliverance—call solemn assemblies, turn to Him
and rend, or tear, our hearts in repentance, and believe in His
kindness and mercy. His answer for today's crises is the same as
what He spoke in Joel's generation when a Babylonian invasion was
encroaching. This is the clearest passage in the Word that describes
what God desires of the Church in times of local or national crisis.
As the global drama unfolds at the end of the age, the Body of
Christ has a clear road map. What a holy boldness this brings! We
can act with certainty in times of crisis.

Solemn Assemblies

We must be clear on the importance of corporate dimensions
of prayer and fasting. Joel identified this critical component as he
entreated the people to corporately cry out to God. This passage,
along with Joel 1:13-14, emphasizes the scope of this gathering.
The situation demanded that all the people, including the elders, the
children, and even the bridegrooms and the brides, be summoned
to this holy convocation. Implicit in this comprehensive call is the
sacred and sober nature of the assembly.

When we gather in the wake of calamity or in preparation for
what is impending, we must do so in a posture of humility and
lamentation. Through the prophet Joel, the Lord instructs people
to fast and mourn, and those who minister to Him to weep in
intercession all night long. It is not enough to casually meet and

casually pray. When disaster strikes, and as we look toward the severity of the days ahead, we must set aside all distractions and throw our hearts into groaning and travail in one accord, beseeching the Lord to have mercy.

Rending Our Hearts

In order for fasting and corporate intercessory worship to be effective, it must be embraced by a wholehearted people. To rend means to tear something violently or forcibly. When we violently tear our hearts away from areas of sin, we line up with what God requires. Traditionally, ancient peoples would tear their garments to show their grief and desperation. When God desires the tearing of the heart (Joel 2:13), He is speaking of a radical, spiritual violence toward all that separates us from Him (Matt. 11:12). Joel essentially cried out, "Tear your heart open! Spare not! If there is an issue in your life that quenches the Holy Spirit, get rid of it!" Speaking symbolically of this radical tearing, Jesus said, "If your right eye causes you to sin, pluck it out ... and if your right hand causes you to sin, cut it off ... " (Matt. 5:29-30). He was talking about a radical pursuit of righteousness that painfully tears the heart in the process of repentance. In other words, we are to forsake all compromise, no matter what the cost.

As Westerners, we hope for a wholeheartedness that is gentle, easy and tame, but there is usually pain involved in cooperating with the Lord to pull out the root system of bondage in our lives. Some would prefer not to have to change their lifestyle or the way they spend time in their quest for freedom and holiness. We want the Lord to cause our problems to evaporate without any cost or struggle—without the pain of tearing our hearts. We do not mind fasting a few meals or giving a few hours to cry out in the prayer room, but we usually overlook the necessity of tearing our hearts because we don't want the pain of such an intimate, personal rending.

God is against much of what the Church labels as having our "liberty in God's grace." Many of the "liberties" that the Church fights for are the very things God is fighting against. The ways we spend time and money; the ways we seek honor; the ways we speak, relate and show our bitterness—all show evidence that we have not torn away from that which hinders us in God.

God the Father's heart was torn when He gave His only Son as a sacrifice for sin, and it continues to be torn in His patient longsuffering with His people as they refuse to respond with repentance. Jesus tore His heart when He went to the cross. It is not a mystery why God wants us to tear our hearts in love for Him. He tears His own heart in His pursuit after us; He has proven that He does not love us in a detached, distant way. To fully enter into this love, and to participate in the fullness of fasting and prayer in solemn assemblies, our own hearts must be torn.

Have Confidence in God's Kindness and Mercy

"Return to the Lord ... for He is gracious and merciful, slow to anger, and of great kindness; and He relents from doing harm. Who knows if He will turn and relent ... ?" (Joel 2:13-14). Joel summoned the people to return to the Lord, giving five reasons why they could have confidence even in their weakness: God is *gracious, merciful, slow to anger, of great kindness* and *He relents from doing harm.* He desires to make a way of deliverance. The knowledge of God's heart for us gives us courage to tear our hearts in repentance. If we take one step toward Him, He will take ten steps toward us.

"He has not dealt with us according to our sins, nor punished us according to our iniquities" (Ps. 103:10). The Lord graciously evaluates us differently than anyone else does. He remembers our frailty, that we are but dust (Ps. 103:14). He is not like a harsh military leader or an angry coach who rejects any form of weakness. "Who is a God like You, pardoning iniquity ... because He delights in mercy" (Mic. 7:18). The Lord delights in mercy. One of God's favorite things to do as He leads the universe is to observe our heart responses as we encounter His relentless mercy. He delights in what is awakened in us when we understand that He tenderly gives us a new start after each of our many failures.

"Do you despise the riches of His goodness and kindness ... it leads to repentance ... " (Rom. 2:4). The Lord has great goodness and kindness in His dealings with us. When we believe in God's kindness, we can confidently press through to full repentance because we do not feel that God despises us in the process. We ask Him to help us repent because we know He is on our side. Our repentance will never be met with rejection. Out of the vast repository of kindness in His heart, God relents from sending judgment when His people turn to Him. God delights in relenting from judgment. He honors our free will. He wants to send blessing to us in place of harm, but will not do so unless the people cry out to Him.

We must understand the two stages that are involved when God decrees a judgment. First, the decree is established in the heavenly court. Second, it is either canceled or issued. "Gather yourselves together ... before the decree is issued ... before the Lord's fierce anger comes upon you ... Seek the Lord, all you meek of the earth ... it may be that you will be hidden *(protected from judgment)* in the day of the Lord's anger" (Zeph. 2:1-3).

God is willing to relent, or to cancel the decree of judgment, instead of issuing it. In response to our prayer, God changes what He releases in our lives. The story of the destruction of Sodom and Gomorrah contains one example of God's willingness to relent. Upon learning of God's intentions to judge the city, Abraham asked the Lord if He would spare the inhabitants if there were only fifty righteous people in it. The Lord said that He would. Abraham kept pressing the question, reducing the number of righteous people each time, until he finally asked, "If there were only ten righteous in the city, would You spare them?" Again, the Lord told Abraham that He would (Gen. 18:22-33). Yet not even ten righteous people were found, and the cities were destroyed.

The story of Nineveh is another example of God's willingness to relent. Jonah proclaimed that God was going to judge the city. The city repented and God saved the entire city (Jonah 3:4-10).

Scripture abundantly testifies to the fact that the course of events, or even their end results, can be changed (Gen. 18:22-32; Ex. 32: 9-14; 2 Sam. 12:15-23, 24:10-16; 2 Chr. 34:22-28; Jer. 18:7-10, 51:6-8; Ezek. 18:21, 22, 28, 33:10-14; Dan. 4:27; Amos 5:1-3,14-15, 7:1-6; Zeph. 2:1-3; Hab. 3:16-19; Jon. 3:4-10; Mal. 3:16-4:6).

I encourage everyone to study the Book of Joel. It is a short Old Testament book that has great relevance to the Church in light of coming worldwide revival and crisis. I refer to Joel as a "mini Book of Revelation." I have written a syllabus on Joel, which covers each verse in the Book. It further develops the themes of fasting and prayer in light of what will come to the Earth.

CHAPTER TWELVE

The Global Bridegroom Fast: Establishing a Joel 2 Culture

Responding to the invitation to enter into a lifestyle of fasting out of longing for our heavenly Bridegroom, and understanding the necessity of solemn assemblies in light of the coming global crisis, the International House of Prayer in Kansas City has established the Global Bridegroom Fast. At the beginning of each month, the entire staff and anyone else who would like to participate gathers for three days of corporate intercessory worship, prayer and fasting.

In Kansas City we convene the first Monday, Tuesday and Wednesday of every month, and for seven days in December, which totals forty days of fasting each year. Our corporate intercession is centered around six 2-hour prayer meetings each day (6 a.m., 10 a.m., 4 p.m., 8 p.m., midnight and 4 a.m.) It is a blessed time, set aside to mourn the absence of Jesus, to cry out for His return, to remember our first love, and to cry out for unprecedented activity of the Holy Spirit to be released here and abroad.

Though an answer to the mandate of Scripture, the Global Bridegroom Fast was initiated by the Lord when He spoke prophetically to our leadership in January of 2002. He instructed the community of believers here to embrace an ongoing commitment to monthly sacred assemblies until Jesus returns, and to summon the Body of Christ all over the world to do the same.

Global Bridegroom Fast: A Worldwide Solemn Assembly

This worldwide call is not a call for people to join a specific structure or ministry associated with IHOP-KC. On the contrary, it is an invitation to all believers scattered throughout the world to rend their hearts and give themselves to a radical lifestyle of fasting that is rooted in the affections of Jesus and His imminent return. The vision is for 100 million believers around the world to assemble in their localities and contend for a breakthrough of the power of God and for unprecedented revival to touch the nations, especially Israel.

Although the particular format is not paramount, we do humbly invite those who accept this vision to hold assemblies concurrent with our schedule for the power of unified intercession. Of course, the leadership of the various gatherings has freedom to adjust the prayer model and emphases as the Lord leads. More important than the format is a wholehearted commitment to Jesus and to the biblical values described in the previous chapters. Maintaining absolutely no organizational oversight of these meetings, IHOP-KC will simply champion the cause and provide whatever resources we can to encourage the abandoned pursuit of Christ through fasting and prayer. Imagine 100 million saints praying and fasting at the same time, and focusing on the revelation of the Lord Jesus as the Bridegroom! The Lord is raising up a global concert of prayer and fasting throughout the nations. The result will be an open Heaven over the Body of Christ and the nation of Israel, like the vision Jacob experienced in Gen. 28:10.

Establishing a Joel 2 Culture

The monthly Global Bridegroom Fast is a critical endeavor that the Lord has strategically beckoned us to enter. Yet the state of the Western Church is such that far more is necessary than a monthly gathering. We must understand this type of fasting as a way of life. A time is quickly approaching that is so perilous and severe that we have no frame of reference with which to understand it, apart from receiving revelation from God. The devil is orchestrating the greatest release of evil ever known in human history. Deception and sin will fill the Earth as never before, and the Church must have a radical response—we must be positioned together in continual prayer and fasting the way the Lord has prescribed in Scripture. The entire culture of the Church must dramatically change if it is to remain steadfast and blameless at the Lord's coming.

The great conflict at the end of the age will be between two houses of prayer. Both houses come from the loins of Abraham—the house of Jacob (who God renamed Israel) and the house of Ishmael. In other words, the end-time Body of Christ and the house of Islam, each functioning as a house of prayer, are on the path for a great collision just before Jesus returns. More than 100 million Muslims worldwide participate in Ramadan, which is 30 days of fasting at the end of each year, usually in November. They pursue a religious purity to gain favor and power with Allah. Other religions, including Hinduism and Buddhism, practice extreme fasting and prayer on a regular basis as well.

The Body of Christ must have a response that matches and even exceeds the dedication of false religions. God is raising up the Church as His hammer in the Spirit to contend with the Ramadan fast and the belief system behind it (Is. 41:15). The Holy Spirit is arousing the Church to shake off compromise and passivity, and to contend for truth to pervade the nations. This requires that we heed the message given by Joel, the call to solemn assemblies, as a normal part of our spiritual culture. In order to respond rightly, we as the western Church need an entirely new way of life to sweep through the Body of Christ. We need to live in continual prayer and fasting. The practical dimensions of gathering together for the

Bridegroom Fast represent the entire lifestyle we must embrace as the Body of Christ—the lifestyle outlined by Joel.

Hear and Give Ear

"Hear this, you elders, and give ear, all you inhabitants of the land! Has anything like this happened in your days, or even in the days of your fathers?" (Joel 1:2). It takes the work of the Holy Spirit for our hearts to receive the revelation of this message. Whether in Joel's day or in ours, its wisdom does not change. Its first exhortation is to "hear and give ear," which means to diligently study the book of Joel. Its long-term core message is that the glory of God in revival is coming, along with the crisis of the Antichrist and the Great Tribulation. Joel tells us that during this time, wholeheartedness—a fasted lifestyle—can make a difference, because God is kind and releases blessing in the midst of crisis if His people will seek Him.

Joel challenges the people to "hear," which means they need to lead lifestyles that enhance hearing. We must "give ear" in order to commit to going deeply into the message. This hearing does not come automatically because we are Christians. It requires an intentional, deliberate cultivation of the revelation of the Joel message. In order to hear clearly we need the spirit of revelation (Eph. 1:17).

Jesus made this same appeal to the seven churches mentioned in Revelation, saying, "Him who has ears, let him hear" (Rev. 2:7; 3:6). Jesus was saying in essence, "Pay close attention, because it takes God's help to really hear God's Word." Be careful with the information you receive. If God does not help you hear it, you will end up explaining it away or forgetting it. The end-time message is offensive to our flesh; we naturally resist what challenges our comfort zones. God's instruction for us to hear, to cultivate understanding, is essential. If we experience an initial stirring by the end-time message, we must pursue it until our hearts are gripped with revelation. This message must become a living understanding in our heart.

Another way to say this is that we must "eat the scroll," digesting its truth until it becomes part of us (Ezek. 3:1; Rev. 10:9). If we do not feed our spirit on the message, the initial inspiration we experience by hearing it will quickly evaporate. We pray, "Lord, I will not be content until my heart is burning with revelation so that I live differently." Just like the disciples on the road to Emmaus, we want our hearts to burn within us at the opening of the Scriptures (Luke 24:32).

The Coming Crisis is Unprecedented and Unfamiliar

"Has anything like this happened in your days, or even in the days of your fathers?" (Joel 1:2). Joel began by emphasizing the *unprecedented magnitude* of what was happening. He asked, in essence, "Have you seen anything like this? Do you think this is normal?" If a coming event is unprecedented, it is so unfamiliar to our minds that we don't easily understand it. Our generation is entering a new season on the divine calendar that will result in huge changes on the Earth. God's glory and judgments will shake everything that can be shaken. We are in a unique time period for which we have no frame of reference; its unfamiliarity is part of the difficulty of preparing for it. Most people do not really think about living through the events recorded in the Book of Revelation.

As of today, the great crisis has not begun; we only see small tokens of what is ahead. Yet even now we must not yield to a scoffing spirit of unbelief about Jesus' coming. 2 Peter 3:3-4 warns, "Scoffers will come in the last days, walking according to their own lusts, and saying, 'Where is the promise of His coming? For since the fathers fell asleep, all things continue as they were from the beginning of creation.'"

The scoffers Peter foresaw will be both inside the Church and outside of it. Their worldview will come not from the revelation of Scripture but from their lusts or their wishful thinking. Not willing to let their money, pleasure or power be disrupted, they will deem the lifestyle God prescribed in His Word to be extreme and unnecessary, and the message of the End-Times to be false or unbiblical. Their unbelief and cynicism will motivate them to say, "Where is the promise of His coming?" In other words, "Where is the coming revival and where is the coming judgment?" These scoffers will perpetuate the lie that everything will continue as it always has. They willfully forget that God rules His Kingdom and the universe by His Word (2 Pet. 3:5), and what His Word says will surely come to pass.

What we as believers in the Western world must be alerted to is that truly we do not realize how greatly influenced we are by the scoffing spirit of our culture and the age in which we live. Because we don't imagine ourselves as those who participate in forthright "scoffing" about the Lord's return, we can quickly disregard this exhortation of Peter as not personally applicable. This is crafty deception from the enemy. Even without loud mockery of the Second Coming, we are not immune to the residue of this spirit, which permeates our culture and many of our mindsets. It clutters our thinking and diminishes our fervency, leaving us unknowingly with a dulled spirit.

Our dilemma is that we live under a spiritual fog while we think our skies are clear—we think we are unaffected by something that in truth has many strongholds in our thinking and our way of life. Things are not okay and we do not know it. Things are desperately wrong as the Earth is under the sway of the evil one and is weighed down with rage against God and anger against His ways. For the moment, much sleeps beneath the surface, but the delay does not make what is dormant any less real. The world has been lured to sleep under a false sense of peace as if we were hypnotized by the darkness of this age.

As the crescendo of human history builds at the end of the age, the people of Earth, including us in the Church, are saturated by this seduction and sleep in it. We must be delivered from this. Something is coming, the likes of which mankind has never seen. We don't know that it *will* be in our day; all we know is that it's coming and that the spirit of the age is in full force. Unless we vigorously posture ourselves to mourn for the Bridegroom and come together to fast and intercede, we will be deceived and lured into sleep by the evil one, and thus be caught unaware in the hour of the Lord's return. This is why we cannot romanticize our spiritual state nor neglect the Lord's urgent beckoning to hear His Word.

The Church in the Western world is not yet convinced of what is coming. We have what I call the ostrich syndrome. We put our heads in the ground and hope it will all just go away. Will God change His plans if we simply remain ignorant? No, what is written in the Word of God is not going to go away. It will come to pass whether we are prepared or not. If the locust plague of Joel 1 and the military crisis of Joel 2 is unfamiliar to us, what about the Book of Revelation? The events recorded in Revelation are entirely unfamiliar to us. Has anything like this ever happened? It is completely new ground. The greatest revival and the greatest disaster the world has ever known are around the corner. Our best days and our worst days are swiftly approaching.

Noah is a premier example of someone who responded rightly to God in an unprecedented hour of judgment. He embraced a prophetic message that was totally unfamiliar to him. God told him it would rain for forty days. Noah didn't know what rain was; it had never rained before. Until that time, God watered the ground from below. When Noah told people that water would come from the sky, they rejected his message and undoubtedly mocked him. Everyone knew water came up from the ground, not down from the sky.

The Bible says, however, that strange as it must have been to him, when Noah heard this message from God he was "moved with godly fear" (Heb. 11:7). He followed through with a radical lifestyle change. He gave his time and energy to cutting wood and building an ark—for more than one hundred years. Imagine, eighty years into building his boat, his friends must have said, "Noah, are you sure you heard right?" There was no sign of rain. But Noah was so convinced of the word of the Lord that it changed everything about his life. The way he spent time, money and energy was never the same. Jesus likened the last days to the generation of Noah (Matt. 24:37-39). Something unprecedented is coming to our generation; like Noah, we also must dramatically change the way we live today.

Leaders Must Lead

"Hear this, you elders, and give ear, all you inhabitants of the land!" (Joel 1:2). The mandate to "hear" begins with spiritual leadership. Leaders must "give ear." In other words, they must give themselves to this message. They must get on their knees before God with an open Bible and begin to study and meditate on what the Old Testament prophets say will happen in the generation that the Lord returns. The "inhabitants of the land" will tune in when their leaders hear and enter into fasting and prayer, leading by example (Joel 1:2). The greatest gift that God can give a nation is to raise up leaders who have a spirit of revelation and the grace of fasting and prayer.

America's greatest crisis is not the sin occurring in Hollywood or in Washington, D.C. It is not what is happening in the sin-centers of our major cities. The biggest problem in America is that the Church is mostly being led by leaders who are without a spirit of revelation, who do not understand the urgency of the hour, and who are without a spirit of fasting and prayer. This was one of the greatest tragedies during the crisis of September 11, 2001. The leaders of the Church did not know how to respond or address the events of September 11. When this problem is rectified, leaders who walk in the anointing of God will address other necessary issues. The biblical progression is for God's leaders to first hear what the Spirit is saying; then the people will earnestly give ear to it. God's people as a whole only do what their leaders do.

Proclaim the Message

Joel 1:3 tells us that, after we give ear to the message, we must tell others. We must not only hear and be gripped by this message;

we must also proclaim it. The price we will pay for boldly telling the truth can be seen in the persecutions that the Old Testament prophets endured. They were criticized, ostracized, imprisoned and killed. The Lord honors the courage and faith that it takes to proclaim the Joel 2 end-time message, and He will give us more revelation and authority if we faithfully use what He entrusts to us. Jesus quoted Joel 1:2 when He said to His disciples, "If anyone has ears to hear, let him hear ... Take heed what you hear. With the same measure you use, it will be measured to you; and to you who hear, more will be given. For whoever has, to him more will be given; but whoever does not have, even what he has will be taken away from him" (Mark 4:23-25).

Establish a Dynamic Spiritual Culture – Tell the Children

"Tell your children about it, let your children tell their children, and their children another generation" (Joel 1:3). After calling the elders to hear and all the inhabitants of the land to give ear, Joel gives them a mandate to pass this message on to four generations. The elders and people must tell their children, who tell their children, who in turn tell the next generation. Every child must hear this message clearly and grow up understanding end-time realities. It should be as normal for them to hear about the end of the age as it was for Noah's three sons to hear that a flood was coming.

We do not want our children to grow up dumbfounded at what is coming or indifferent to it. Our children must know that the coming Day is both great and terrible; they must know how to partner with a kind and loving God right now and in that day by living lifestyles of prayer with fasting. A child's spirit is moldable and teachable, like wet cement. Whatever we write on these open spirits, this wet cement, they will receive as true and normal.

Adults can struggle for years to get free from wrong paradigms about God that were formed in their youth. We want the pliable hearts of our children to be wet cement that sets with truth imbedded in them. They will believe that an unprecedented evil along with unprecedented revival is coming. They will understand that an evil, worldwide Antichrist regime will arise, more powerful and cruel than any political or military coalition that the world has never known. But they will also know that Jesus is returning to rule and reign as King over all the Earth. In preparation for this hour, they must understand and believe that fasting and prayer are normal for God's people. They will remember what their moms and dads did—they gathered together for fasting and prayer.

(Dana speaking) My husband, Matt, and I had our first child a year ago, a little girl named Madison. We are gripped with this urgent necessity of redefining what her "normal" is according to what is true in the Word of God, not according to the onslaught of deception that fills our culture and the age we live in. Perhaps the most difficult part of the process of teaching our children is the constant personal realignment necessary in our own hearts to swim against a raging current of comfort, ease and passivity. We must sustain urgency in our own lives, not just the lives of our children.

What is our *normal* will become her *normal*, no matter what that looks like. Urgency and a lifestyle of mourning for the Bridegroom is not something that we sign up for one day and it is finalized in our hearts. Rather, it is something that we have to recommit to doing every single day—shaking ourselves out of lethargy and passivity by the grace of God. This is our heart for our daughter, our own lives, the community of believers we live among, and for the Body of Christ in our day.

A spiritual culture is established in the Church based on what we teach our children. Our children will teach the same to their children. By the time four generations have been taught, a people will exist who believe in the message. It will be considered normal to believe and to act in the ways the Word of God says. Establishing this dynamic spiritual culture according to the Joel 2 message drives out the scoffing spirit that is filled with complacency (2 Pet. 3:3-4).

The spiritual culture of the Body of Christ is filled right now with a scoffing and complacent spirit. The complacent spirit has taken such deep root in the leadership of the Church right now that it is considered extreme to believe the Word of God about the End Times. We must in faith believe what God says in His Word. God said it, I believe it, and that settles it for me! Our children must be raised in a spiritual atmosphere of faith and wholeheartedness. In other words, *prayer and fasting is to be the predominate spiritual culture of the end-time Church.* This is what God wanted when He commanded all to "tell the children ... " (Joel 1:3). Imagine how different a day of calamity would look if the young and old together wore filled with understanding and might in the inner man!

It is vital that the Church expend her resources, both human and financial, to raise up children who are equipped to walk out the Joel message. I so thank God for Lenny and Tracy LaGuardia, who serve on the IHOP senior leadership team. They lead the team that trains the adults in our spiritual family to equip the children to walk out the message of the Book of Joel. They have served God's purpose with the children for more than 25 years. I have known and watched them for most of these 25 years. Their vision and consistency to raise up children who move in the power of God is amazing to me.

For these many years, they have held on to the vision of equipping children to move in all that God will give the Body of Christ in this hour. They left a large salary at a mega church to raise their own support as intercessory missionaries in order to join the IHOP staff. I asked them why they were willing to give up so much. They said that they count it a privilege to give up anything to equip children in a community of people who take prayer with fasting seriously enough to contend together for a breakthrough in the power of God. I believe that God is raising up an army of spiritual dads and moms who will take seriously the challenge to cultivate the spiritual culture described in the Book of Joel. The Spirit and the Bride cry, "Maranatha!" Come quickly, Lord Jesus.

For more information about the Book of Joel, see Mike Bickle's study guide, *"Studies in the Book of Joel."*

1

onething

Onething is more than a conference.

It is a ministry committed to seeing a great awakening in the Body of Christ as the hearts of men and women come alive to the true nature of God.

Onething is a young adult ministry based at the International House of Prayer in Kansas City, Missouri. We at Onething have a specific message and carry a mandate to call young adults to return to their primary purpose in this life: loving Jesus. We endeavor to assist young adults in walking out the first commandment to love the Lord with all of their hearts, minds, souls and strength and to pursue a wholehearted passion for Jesus.

Our desire is for the truth of the Man Jesus to pierce hearts, remove chains of bondage, open eyes to understanding, revive complacent hearts, and ultimately cause young adults to become wholehearted lovers of Jesus Christ.

ONE THING HAVE I DESIRED, AND THAT WILL I SEEK ...
PSALM 27:4

WHAT DO YOU DESIRE?

www.IHOP.org

WHAT IS THE IHOP-KC MISSIONS BASE?

It is an international missions organization committed to **Prayer** (intercession, worship, healing, prophesying, etc.), **Fasting** (covering 365 days a year) and the **Great Commission** (proclaiming Jesus to all nations with power as the way to establish His **justice** in the earth). Our work includes equipping and sending missionaries as dedicated intercessors and anointed messengers working to see revival in the Church and a Great Harvest among the lost.

IHOP-KC MISSIONS VISION STATEMENT

To call forth, train and mobilize **worshipping intercessors** who operate in the forerunner spirit as End-Time prophetic messengers. To establish a 24 hour a day Prayer Room in Kansas City as a perpetual solemn assembly that **"keeps the sanctuary"** by gathering corporately to fast and pray in the spirit of the Tabernacle of David as God's **primary method** of establishing justice (full revival unto the Great Harvest). To send out teams to plant Houses of Prayer in the nations **after** God grants a breakthrough of His power in Kansas City. The Forerunner spirit operates in God's grace in context to the fasted lifestyle (Mt. 6) and prepares others to live in wholehearted love by proclaiming the beauty of Jesus as Bridegroom, King and Judge.

VISITING IHOP ON WEEKENDS

Encounter God Services: Weekends at IHOP-KC – renewal, conviction, refreshing, impartation and equipping are what we pray to be released in these weekend meetings at IHOP-KC. On **Friday nights**, Mike Bickle teaches on themes related to intimacy with God. On **Saturday nights**, he teaches on themes related to the End-Times. On Sundays, join the IHOP-KC staff for worship and teaching. Childcare is available. **One Day seminars** are taught on Saturdays.

See www.IHOP.org for details, visitor's accommodations, and more information on joining our staff or attending our internships or Bible School.

PRAYER, FASTING AND THE GREAT COMMISSION

The Church today needs to be mobilized with continual prayer and fasting to release the harvest of souls waiting to be garnered from among the nations. Mike Bickle's reliable ministry at his Missions Base in Kansas City is helping to answer a great need in this hour.
— Jack W. Hayford, The Church On The Way

The Great Commission needs to be fueled with fiery continual prayer with fasting. Our greatest effectiveness in reaching millions of souls will be seen only as our work is bathed in prayer and fasting. Prayer ministries like Mike Bickle's in Kansas City are important for the completion of the Great Harvest.
— Bill Bright, Campus Crusade for Christ

The Great Harvest needs to be supplied by continual prayer and fasting. Intercessory ministries like Mike Bickle's in Kansas City are vital for the fulfillment of the Great Commission.
— Loren Cunningham, YWAM

As a lifelong missiologist, I cannot help but think that the landscape of humanity will drastically change when the body of Christ actually becomes a House of Prayer. Mike Bickle has risked it all to convince us of this fact. I heartily recommend this amazing work!
— C. Peter Wagner, Leadership Institute

Mike, you are helping fulfill a desire of God's heart for His presence to be enthroned night and day upon a people that love Him. What you are pioneering at the IHOP Missions Base has huge significance for all who labor to reach the nations. May your lamp of worship and prayer continue to shine!
— John Dawson, Youth With A Mission

Spiritual awakening in our nation and world cannot be sustained unless heaven's bowls stay continually filled through worship and intercession. Now more than ever, we need night and day prayer to make a difference! Thanks to Mike Bickle for helping to lead the charge.
— Dutch Sheets

IHOP INTERNSHIPS – 3 MONTH AND 6 MONTH PROGRAMS – ALL AGES

Each internship program has the same basic training components including prayer meetings, classroom training, practical ministry experience, relationships and team building, conferences, practical serving, and training in the Word. Each Training Program regularly participates in prayer meetings in the IHOP-KC Prayer Room, which includes worship team involvement, intercession for revival, personal study and devotional time. Time spent in the Prayer Room ranges from 15 to 25 hours or more weekly. Our training covers a wide range of subjects: Christian foundations, prayer, worship, intimacy with God, Bride of Christ, prophetic, healing, outreach ministry to the lost and poor, etc.

Intro to IHOP – for all ages, married or single is a 3-month training program for those wanting to learn and experience all that IHOP represents (prayer, worship, intimacy, etc).

Simeon Company (age 50 and over) is a 3-month training program for those who refuse to retire in their desire to radically serve Jesus through prayer, fasting, and worship.

'Onething…' internship (Ages 18-25) is a daytime 6-month training program for singers, musicians, intercessors, and evangelists. This program includes housing and 18 meals a week.

Fire in the Night (ages 18-30) is a 3-month training program focused on raising up those who pray through the night (midnight to 6 AM). This program includes housing and 18 meals a week.

Summer Teen Internship is 3-week program in the summer to equip teens in prophetic worship, intercession, and intimacy with Jesus. housing is provided with families of IHOP-KC.

FORERUNNER SCHOOL OF MINISTRY (FSM)

Redefining Theological Education Through Night and Day Prayer
Passion for Jesus : The Forerunner Ministry : Centrality of Scripture :
Community of Believers : 24/7 Intercessory Worship : Evangelism and World Missions :
Ministry in the Power of the Spirit

The Forerunner School of Ministry is a full-time Bible school advancing the prayer, worship, and Missions movement . 1, 2, 3, and 4 year study programs are available. FSM is committed to the Word of God and the power of the Holy Spirit. FSM provides training for worship leaders, preachers, pastors, evangelists, musicians, intercessors.

5 Distinct Schools: School of Apostolic Preaching—School of Worship & Prayer—School of Healing and the Prophetic School of Biblical Studies—School of Missions—Forerunner Music Academy

FORERUNNER MUSIC ACADEMY (FMA)

FMA is a full-time music school that trains musicians and singers to play skillfully and to operate in the prophetic anointing. FMA offers a comprehensive course of high quality musical training in the context of IHOP's night and day prayer and worship. King David understood that prophetic music and songs would release the power of God. He paid 4,000 full-time musicians and hundreds of prophetic singers to gaze day and night upon God as they sang the prayers of Zion. This was their primary occupation in life. They were employed in the Tabernacle of David, which combined worship with intercession that never ceased as it continued 24/7.

VISIT IHOP-KC AT WWW.IHOP.ORG

The International House of Prayer Missions Base website has been designed for ease of browsing. We have incorporated the following branches of our community into one cohesive site:

- IHOP
- Onething
- Children's Equipping Center
- Forerunner School of Ministry
- Forerunner Music Academy
- Joseph Company
- Events & Conferences
- Internships & Training Programs
- Omega Course

It's all located at our familiar and easy to remember address: www.IHOP.org. Whether you are interested in visiting IHOP, receiving the Missions Base Podcast, browsing the bookstore, watching live Webcasts, or enrolling in FSM's online eSchool, the website delivers the information you need and offers many opportunities to feed your heart. With login capabilities that expose you to even more comprehensive IHOP materials, we hope our site will become an ongoing resource for many years to come. Some of the website features include:

- Podcasting
- MP3 Downloads
- Forums
- Free & Subscription-based Webcasts
- Sermon & Teaching Notes
- eSchool Distance Learning
- Internship Applications
- Prayer Room Blogs
- Online Bookstore
- And More!

Visit us soon at www.IHOP.org!